Philemon

T0353262

T&T CLARK STUDY GUIDES TO THE NEW TESTAMENT

Philemon: Imagination, Labor, and Love

Series Editor

Tat-siong Benny Liew, College of the Holy Cross, USA

Philemon

Imagination, Labor, and Love

Robert Paul Seesengood

Bloomsbury T&T Clark
An imprint of Bloomsbury Publishing Plc

B L O O M S B U R Y
LONDON · OXFORD · NEW YORK · NEW DELHI · SYDNEY

Bloomsbury T&T Clark

An imprint of Bloomsbury Publishing Plc

Imprint previously known as T&T Clark

50 Bedford Square	1385 Broadway
London	New York
WC1B 3DP	NY 10018
UK	USA

www.bloomsbury.com

BLOOMSBURY, T&T CLARK and the Diana logo are trademarks of Bloomsbury Publishing Plc

First published 2017

British Library Cataloguing-in-Publication Data
A catalogue record for this book is available from the British Library.

ISBN: PB: 978-0-5676-7495-1
ePDF: 978-0-5676-7496-8
ePub: 978-0-5676-7497-5

Library of Congress Cataloging-in-Publication Data
A catalog record for this book is available from the Library of Congress.

Series: T&T Clark Study Guides to the New Testament, volume 5

Cover design by clareturner.co.uk
Cover image © Vince Cavataio/Getty Images

Typeset by Newgen Knowledge Works (P) Ltd., Chennai, India.

Contents

Acknowledgments

A heartfelt thank you is owed to Tat-siong Benny Liew for the invitation to take on this project and for his near limitless patience and editorial vision. I am also grateful to Trudy Prutzman, whose administrative skills have been wonderful, and to Justine Ellie Smith, an effective research assistant who improved the references, citations, and bibliography. I am grateful for generous colleagues who were willing to read, comment on, or listen to my ideas, particularly Joseph Marchal, Jennifer Bird, and my Albright colleagues Victor Forte and Samira Mehta. As always, I'm deeply grateful to the inexhaustible Jennifer Koosed, my collaborator in all things. I am a better scholar because of the opportunity to read over her shoulder, and a better writer because of her willingness to read over mine.

Portions of this book, particularly the Introduction and Chapter 2, were presented at faculty and department forums at Albright College. Comments and questions made the book both stronger in argument and clearer in focus. Chapter 1 was written with the assistance of an Albright College Summer Research Grant. I am particularly grateful to Sandra Stump of Albright College's F. W. Gingrich Library, for collection development and interlibrary loan.

I was bereaved during the writing of this book, which was in part delayed, by the untimely loss of two colleagues: Elizabeth Kiddy, professor of history and Latin American studies, Albright College, and Rosemary Deegan, director of the Wilbur F. Gingrich Library. This book is dedicated to the memory of many pleasant conversations with each about books and what they might mean.

Introduction : On Reading Lost Letters

In my first year of undergraduate college, I found a note lodged in a library book: a torn corner of cheap, yellow, "legal pad" paper, roughly three-by-five inches in size, horizontally lined in blue with a red vertical left-margin mark, written in two hands, one in black ink and the other in pencil. The first (in ink) read: "It will begin at 3:00." The second (in pencil): "Today is November 13." I found it while writing an essay for a course in American history. I cannot recall the essay, its thesis, or even much of its subject beyond a general, "undergradese" survey of taxation issues leading up to the American Revolution. I cannot recall the book at all. I can no longer remember much about taxation issues leading up to the American Revolution. I can recall the note perfectly, however. In my mind's eye, I can see the paper, the script, the way that the paper was folded once, down the center separating "3:" from "00" and splitting "November" at the first "e." I can see the gap of an inch or so between the two sentences, each sentence left-justified, as well as the blank space of nearly a third of the right-hand side of the note. The first line was written within one set of blue-lined margins; the second scrawled across two.

I kept the note. By my reckoning, I had the note in my haphazard stewardship for about seven or eight years. I used it as a bookmark of my own. For years, certainly through the whole of my undergraduate career, my time at seminary, and my graduate work beyond, it would pop up in my life, appearing mysteriously inside a book I had once used or read or simply carried around as an academic talisman, a book destined soon to be laid aside. My life with the note was a series of discovery and loss, of finding and forgetting. I do not know exactly when the note and I parted company, though I assume we have. I have not seen it for over a decade now, and I no longer wonder if I will one day discover it lodged in some arcane volume that sits on my shelves. It is possible that it is still here, somewhere, perhaps in this very room, but I don't really think so. I have long suspected that I left it in a library book myself, or, perhaps, in a book which I decided to sell or give away because of disuse. In my imagination, the note now circulates somewhere around Princeton, New Jersey, taunting some other scholar as it once did me.

It takes very little to distract a writer in the early stages of work. This note would stall me, sometimes for as long as an hour, every time I found it. I wondered what "it" was, and why it was to begin at 3:00. Am or pm? Did it begin on time? Was it a party? A movie? A class, a lab or a lecture? Or was it a game, a date? Perhaps something more dire? Recalling the Bible-centered ferocity of my childhood world, I sometimes imagined it was a mistaken declaration of something apocalyptic. Why would someone write the day's date? Was it an answer to a question, perhaps a furtive note passed during a class or supervised study hall? Was it a reminder to someone distracted or ill? In my imagination I recalled the signs posted in my mother's hospital room, gentle and gracious reminders of an outside world busy at its tasks: "Today is …" Who were the authors? Students or professors? In school when I was or years before? Alive or dead? Male or female? I imagined— looking closely at the note, the first line in print and the second in cursive— that the handwriting looked somehow "masculine" to me. The writing by the second hand also seemed to slant to the right, suggesting a right-handed author. That by the first was much more vertical, perhaps a lefty? (Though the precise writing, the print, the use of the colon to clarify expression of an hour all might equally suggest a generally precise person.) I wondered if the two authors knew one another. I wondered if this was a part of a larger conversation. I wondered, at times, if it was conspiratorial. I would imagine it as part of a brief but furtive conversation:

Second hand: Today is November 13.
First hand (in answer): [Oh, then,] It [whatever "it" was] begins at 3:00.

Or, perhaps, just the opposite:

First hand: It begins at 3:00.
Second hand (emphatic): [No!] Today is November 13 [so, it begins at some other time or, perhaps, not at all].

Other possibilities proliferate (as I said, "easily distracted"), and I've not even scratched the surface about what "it" might be. Surely, the basis for a good novel is somewhere in this imagined dialogue.

I wondered, in later years, if it might not be the case that the two authors were as separated from one another in time and unknown to each other as I was to them. Perhaps one of the hands had jotted a reminder note to her/himself and left it in a book; the second hand discovered the note, like I did, and made a reminder of her/his own. Perhaps later s/he used the note as a bookmark and, after the assignment or project was long forgotten (and, though I cannot remember the book, I do remember enough that I cannot expect it to be a book often read for pleasure), the paper was left for me to find. Whenever I rediscovered the note, I would take it, read it, wonder about it, and lay it aside for a while. Once or twice I myself was tempted to write a quick note on it—a page reference or some other arcane fact—but I stopped myself. I wonder who found the note after me, if anyone has (if, indeed, it is not somewhere still hidden inside my own library). Did s/he find it mysterious as well? Did s/he keep it as well or did s/he throw it away or use it as a marker in turn before leaving it behind again in some other book? Did s/he simply scavenge it for a note in turn (and, indeed, there is no reason not to)? Would s/he wonder or even imagine that the note had traveled over a thousand miles in seven years? Had it traveled as far or further before it came to me?

Two sentences, so specific and completely indicative (declaratory even), but so completely insensible and vague because of their lack of provenance. Perfectly sensible and correct, they are now meaningless. They most certainly have a history and a "meaning." Their authors almost certainly had an intended purpose or meaning behind their composition (I long ago decided that it was more Borgesian than probable to think that this otherwise "meaningless" note was intentionally secreted in a book for me to find and wonder about). The problem is not at all that the language of the note is unclear, obscure, difficult, or challenging. Yet, because of their lost provenance, the lines of the note are now, ultimately, meaningless.

In time, the note took on a second level of meaning-making for me. Like the rediscovery of a long-forgotten photo of oneself, perhaps from childhood, discovering the note in a book would remind me again of old projects, old inquiries, old infatuations. I would remember my own history with the note and its successive appearances. I would remember the places I once worked—studies, library carrels, offices. I would remember the people I was with—partners, teachers, colleagues, classmates. Sometimes, for days, there would be twinges of nostalgia; sometimes, perhaps most of the time, the note simply inspired a snort and a smile.

Today, the note may lie dormant on a library shelf. It may be held by some other caretaker. It may lie rotting on the ground somewhere or in a landfill. It may have been long ago recycled. The physical note is gone. I use the note, however, as a metaphor, an analogy for my students. It is now a thought-experiment that precedes a (now somewhat canned) lecture that introduces the section on the Pauline Letters in my Introduction to the New Testament course.

The issues surrounding the interpretation of this simple note differ from the criticism of the Bible in general, and Paul's letters in particular, only in scale and not in essence. To interpret the note, we need a provenance, a setting-in-life, a point of origin. All communication requires a context for meaning; no writing is self-contained. At minimum, a piece of writing must acknowledge certain norms about grammar and vocabulary. In order for a writing, any writing, to have meaning, the reader must have a (re)constructed context.

Context tells us how to interpret words. At the most basic level, to read a document, we must know its language. But more than a working knowledge of the language, we also need to be aware of nuances to meaning that change or develop among various communities of language users and across time. Imagine, for example, how differently even a native English speaker might interpret the sentence, "She teasingly told me I was much too gay," if it was written in 1917 or 2017. Nuances in language—including denotative and connotative meanings, particular usages, slangs, so on and so forth—are all products of context. We may deduce the context of a piece of writing by examining closely how it uses language, but changing the context presumed behind a piece of writing—that is, changing its provenance—also changes the "meaning" derived from that writing.

Context helps us interpret setting and plot. This is particularly key for writings like letters or epistles. Recall, for example, how many (equally plausible) scenarios "behind" my found note could be constructed. Notice how each change in context—each location or setting in life presumed behind the document—changes its meaning. Writings also make reference to "insider" terminology, private jokes, current events (political and cultural), other people, and much more. Knowing the historical, geographical, or chronological context for a piece of writing helps us interpret it. Knowing, as well, the "plot" assumed in or behind a piece of writing is also key to its interpretation.

Knowing to whom a piece of writing refers (or whom it invokes or references) also helps us interpret. Even if the author and (presumed) audience are not famous or broadly known, having some sense of who they are—when and where they lived, what their occupations might be, their education, their sophistication with language, their life experiences—factors into interpretation.

Most of these points (and one could go on) seem rather obvious, and they are. Yet many readers are naïve to how little of this information we have about and behind biblical texts. As any instructor of the New Testament or Hebrew Bible knows, much of the actual content of biblical text is inscrutable to the modern reader. The Bible presumes familiarity with a great deal of ancient history. It uses language in both conventional and idiosyncratic ways. Translation obscures the fact that many biblical books use words and grammar in startling manners. The Bible makes reference to cultural and historical events now largely forgotten, remembered only by avid Bible readers and ancient historians.

Reconstruction of the Bible's "background" is both helped and hindered by the Bible's "foreground." The Bible is a book read by many who revere it as an inspired message from God and as the substance of their personal religious faith and devotion. This reverence affects the way that the Bible has been inherited. Some people read the Bible with the clear intention of dislodging the book from its vaulted place. Many read the Bible seeking what we might learn from it regarding ancient customs, history, and values. Everyone reads the Bible with some personal context—of faith or without faith, as a scholar or not as a scholar—as well as for unique needs and interests.

Focusing now on the New Testament, we need to realize that we do not have the original copy (the "autograph") of any New Testament book. Our oldest manuscripts of a New Testament book are a century or more later than its first composition, and these early manuscripts preserve only a tiny fraction of the New Testament. Who "found," verified, and collected the New Testament writings has been long lost to history. We have copies of copies of copies of various New Testament books, all handwritten, no originals, and these copies have no "certificate of authenticity" or copyright or other mark to identify their original setting and contents.

Many beginning students may believe that the context of the New Testament—the "background" of who characters are; what happened in their lives; when, where, and why the books were written—is generally known and has been kept in active memory by long-standing tradition and scholarship. Certainly, some traditions about various New Testament characters and events have been kept alive. The traditions which place the writings in context, traditions that assign authorship and historical setting, are often very old; they are also more pervasive and extensive than we have for any other ancient writing. And yet, their age is still, very often, hundreds of years after the events they say a New Testament text is addressing, and the number of varied (often equally plausible) explanations and traditions also suggests prudent care is better than simply accepting any given tradition as absolute.

Of interpretation, there is no end

In terms of Paul's letters, our earliest manuscript that contains a portion of any writing assigned to Paul is from the late second century. Paul makes reference to letters he has written that are no longer extant (2 Cor. 2.1–4; cf. Col. 4.16). Paul often draws attention to his own handwritten signature (1 Cor. 16.21; Gal. 6.11; Phlm 19; cf. Col. 4.18; 2 Thess. 3.17). Paul's letters seem, in places, to be afraid of the possibility of variant teachings or forged letters circulating under his name (Gal. 1.8–9; cf. 2 Thess. 2.1–2). Some letters from antiquity claim Pauline authorship but are widely known to be fakes; forged letters titled 3 Corinthians and Laodiceans exist. Scholars debate over the authenticity of the thirteen letters found in the New Testament that have been associated with Paul.

The letters attributed to Paul may be divided into three groups: the "undisputed" (Romans, 1 and 2 Corinthians, Galatians, Philippians, 1 Thessalonians and Philemon), where Paul's authorship is almost universally accepted by modern critical scholars; the "disputed" (Ephesians, Colossians, and 2 Thessalonians), where Paul's authorship is under serious debate; and the Pastorals (1 and 2 Timothy and Titus), where Paul's authorship is generally denied (see Roetzel 1998). We don't know at all who collected Paul's letters. Our only source into Paul's "context" or biography is the Book of Acts. Yet, as a biography of Paul, Acts is, at best, incomplete; it doesn't, for example, address events narrated in Paul's own letters or reveal Paul's ultimate fate. If we assume the narrative provided by Acts is generally accurate (and not all scholars do), we still do not know the specific time and context of most of Paul's letters; Acts does not even depict Paul as a letter writer.

To interpret any writing we must have a context. This is particularly true for the interpretation of letters, as we saw with my initial example. Yet, the contexts of Paul's writings were, in its best moments, only partial and mediated by much later tradition(s). The process of interpreting Paul's letters is often one of reconstructing plausible contexts, again much like we saw for the interpretation of our anonymous note. As we reconstruct a context, we are able to (re)construct meanings or interpretations. Our interpretations of what a letter means can, in a sense, "verify" our starting hypotheses on its context; at the very least, they should be resonant with those assumptions. If they are not, they may modify our initial assumption(s) or be modified in turn. Each subsequent round of review and interpretation builds more data, reveals more data, coheres more data; much like completing a crossword puzzle, each "answer" generates or clarifies other "answers."

Yet, if we change the original context, we can also radically change what "works" and what doesn't, that is, what seems more plausible or probable as a reconstructed meaning, in our document. We can, by constructing competing contextual frames, construct competing interpretations or meanings for the text, each of which is equally plausible in its own frame but conceivably contradictory of the other readings.

Church tradition has provided some ideas for Philemon's context, but these are not without their problems, as we shall see. Philemon, on the whole, is both maddeningly short and specific. It mentions specific people and assumes a general context and back-story. Yet no specifics of that context or back-story are provided. Acts is of no help in identifying the individuals named or the precise moment in Paul's career when Philemon was drafted.

Paul, born Saul of Tarsus (on the southern coast of modern Turkey), was a devout Jew; later, as a follower of Jesus, he traveled the Roman world in the rough middle of the first century CE, spreading his understanding of Jesus as the Jewish Messiah foretold by Hebrew Scriptures. Though not one of Jesus's initial followers, Paul supposedly came to faith in Jesus as Messiah because of a vision he had in or around the early 40s CE. For the next 20 years, he dedicated his life to spreading his understanding of Jesus. According to tradition, he died in the mid-60s CE, executed just outside the walls of Rome by order of the emperor.

Well trained in Jewish literature and practice of his day, Paul was a fairly active letter writer, sending letters (formally, "epistles") to various communities of Jesus followers in the Roman world (mostly, large cities surrounding the Aegean Sea). Scholars generally agree that his first letter to a community in the ancient city of Thessalonica (1 Thessalonians) is the earliest surviving document ever written by a Jesus follower. All of Paul's letters predate the composition of the Christian Gospels. Paul, then, is our earliest ancient source for the development of early Christianity and a rare window into the intellectual world of late Second Temple Judaism.

Philemon is one of the shortest documents in the New Testament and the shortest writing to have survived from Paul. It is often associated with the letter to the Colossians. Philemon is a personal document written to one of Paul's friends, a fellow named Philemon. Paul seems to have been

Philemon's teacher at some point, guiding Philemon to faith in Jesus as the Christ, or Jewish Messiah. As the letter unfolds, we learn that Paul, under some form of "house arrest" by the (Roman?) authorities, has met another man named Onesimus. Paul, according to Acts, was frequently arrested and held by local authorities because they viewed his teachings as a threat to the Roman order. It is unclear where or how Onesimus and Paul met. What is clear, however, is that Onesimus has been separated from Philemon and that Onesimus, after meeting Paul, has become a Jesus follower. Philemon and Onesimus seem estranged; yet, Paul is not only sending along news of his current condition in the letter but also sending Onesimus back to Philemon, expressing hopes that the two can reconcile. Paul hopes that their ruptured relationship can be restored as fellow believers in Jesus.

My scholarly work in the past few years has centered around "reception history" of the New Testament, particularly the writings associated with Paul and his later followers. "Reception history" in biblical studies is the examination of how scholars and communities through history have interpreted the writings of the Bible. It examines how various views, opinions, decisions, and conclusions of scholars (and faith communities) who read the Bible were shaped by—and, in their own turn, shaped—what they found in Scripture. It also examines how biblical interpretation is produced by and produces broader cultural, intellectual, ideological, and artistic values and norms.

Philemon will prove, I believe, to be an excellent site for pursuing these interests. There was a keen interest in Philemon among nineteenth-century American clergy (Harrill 2000). In the mid-twentieth century, Philemon became a resource for scholars to reimagine Christian history (Knox 1955; 1959). Since the turn of the twenty-first century, there has been a renewed interest in Philemon among scholars writing in English (Barth and Blanke 2000; Fitzmyer 2000; Nordling 2004; Harris 2010), including some particularly interesting works that explore the effect of Philemon on Western culture and thought (Kreitzer 2008; Jeal 2015). Several studies have also used Philemon to provocatively explore slavery in the Greco-Roman world and its lasting effect on Western culture (Callahan 1998; Callahan, Horsley and Smith 1998; Glancy 2006; Avalos 2011). Philemon is an extraordinary text for these conversations because of its checkered and contentious history of interpretation. Historically, interpretations of Philemon (particularly those that focus on reconstructing the world behind Philemon and the letter's "intent") reveal, perhaps more than those of many other New Testament books, the way a scholar's social setting and needs shape her/his conclusions (Seesengood 2010).

For example, Philemon was hotly debated in the early decades of the nineteenth century in America. Since slavery was widely practiced in the Roman Empire (i.e. Paul's geographic and political context), some assumed that Onesimus was a slave. In fact, as early as the third century CE, early Christian interpreters had begun to suggest that the breach between Onesimus and Philemon was the result of Onesimus's escape. Onesimus, they argued, was Philemon's slave who ran away and somehow met Paul later. According to some, Onesimus was arrested as a fugitive slave and met Paul in prison, where Paul then explained the gospel to him and guided him to become a Jesus follower. The consequences of an escaped slave recaptured were dire. He could face severe beating, being sold to worse labor or even killed. Paul, these ancient interpreters argued, was sending Onesimus back while also appealing to Philemon's better nature; he was asking Philemon not to beat or kill Onesimus, despite what legal options Philemon might have enjoyed.

The fact that Paul seems to be sending back a returned slave was a critical and vital issue in nineteenth-century American public discourse, which was itself torn apart by the issue of slavery in the decades prior to the Civil War. Some argued, very famously, that the American ideals were such that slavery, by its very nature, violated every principle of democracy. America, they argued, must do away with slavery. Others, latching onto ancient arguments about the context of Philemon, countered that slavery was permissible and moral since it was allowed in the New Testament. The New Testament was a critical text for the construction of popular morals and ethics in America of that time. Since the New Testament doesn't condemn it, they argued, the institution of slavery should not be considered to be "immoral." Indeed, they would say, the New Testament goes further. Not only does it not condemn or forbid slavery, Paul's letter to Philemon, they argued, suggests that Paul explicitly endorsed it. Were slavery inherently immoral, they argued, Paul (whom they regarded to be an exemplar of morality as a biblical author) would never have sent Onesimus back home. Abolitionists countered that Philemon wasn't about slavery at all. In v. 16, Paul writes that he is sending Onesimus back "no longer a slave but more than a slave, a beloved brother, especially to me but how much more to you, both in the flesh and in the Lord" (NRSV). The description of Onesimus as a brother "in the flesh," they argued, meant that Onesimus and Philemon were biological siblings. "Slave," they argued, was to be understood as a metaphor. As one might imagine, slavery defenders took the exact opposite argument; "brother," they said, was metaphoric (despite Paul's modifier of "in the flesh," a phrase normally meaning "literally" or "actually"), while "slave" was to be taken literally. The issue could not be more significant. Millions of lives hung in the balance of this one verse in one chapter of one (very short) book of the Bible.

Except, of course, that they didn't really. I would argue that the cultural needs of the time, particularly the political issue of whether or not to endorse slavery in antebellum America, actually shaped both the methods of biblical scholars and the meaning of the very verses that they read. For example, Deut. 23.15 (a key text from a key book of the Bible) expressly forbids the return of an escaped slave. Oddly, this verse was seldom mentioned in the debates over Philemon waged in the American South. Many simply disregarded it altogether; nearly everyone failed to note that the traditional Christian interpretation of Philemon meant that Paul, though born and educated as a devout Jew, was in overt and deliberate violation of that text without giving any explanation at all. Cultural values do not arise exclusively from reading the Bible, despite what anyone claims. Bible reading or interpretation is also shaped by cultural context. There are other moments when readings of Philemon reveal that the needs, concerns, and interests of later interpreters affect their interpretations. The same is true for biblical scholars and their scholarly works.

The plan of this book

This book will proceed in two general movements. The first part of this study will be an orientation that looks at the text, characters, and some of the difficult issues in Philemon (Chapter 1). This overview will prove valuable when we examine the history of interpretation in later chapters. Readers already familiar with Philemon's contents or primarily interested in New Testament interpretation may wish to skip this chapter and return to it later or use it for reference.

In the second part, Chapters 2 through 4, I will explore three readings of Philemon, each with different working assumptions about the context behind the letter and with different understandings of the main characters mentioned in the letter. Chapter 2 will focus on readings that view Onesimus as a slave, Chapter 3 will offer a rethinking of the relationship between Onesimus and Philemon and Chapter 4 will imagine the letter without Paul. Doing this will accomplish two goals. First, it will enable us to review the major hypotheses about the purpose, plan, and, therefore, "meaning" of Philemon. Second, it will demonstrate the larger arguments of this guide: (1) multiple contexts are possible for reading a biblical text; (2) these contexts are largely theoretical; and (3) changing these contexts changes the resulting "meaning" of the text (at times, rather substantially). Reading readings of Philemon will become my device to examine larger issues and methods in New Testament interpretation. Perhaps a final outcome will be a general sense of what reading Philemon could mean to us or teach us today. Some references (often very general) will be provided to encourage further and broader reading, but they are kept to a minimum to allow sustained attention upon the text in front of us. A full bibliography is included at the end.

The first reading will explore the traditional context that is often assumed to be behind Philemon: Onesimus is an escaped slave, once owned by Philemon (a former associate and convert of Paul) but has recently encountered Paul (in prison?) and become a Jesus follower. Paul is sending Onesimus back with veiled hints that Philemon should avoid punishing Onesimus if not actually release or return him to Paul. The second reading will examine the hypothesis most popular among nineteenth-century American abolitionists: Onesimus and Philemon are estranged siblings. Paul, with this hypothesis, is intervening on Onesimus's behalf to quiet a family dispute between novice Christians. It will also explore why the traditional slavery-oriented reading, despite being highly conjectural, was and remains so popular among interpreters. The third reading will explore a relatively new interpretation that Paul is not the author of the letter at all, though this is in some way a return to the nineteenth-century arguments already made by F. C. Baur (1875). At the same time, this third reading is also a very (post)modern and poststructuralist mode of reading, where an original author's intent is immaterial and intertextuality reigns. What emerges from reading the letter adrift, with only the most rudimentary "context" and without a narrative to ground "exegesis"? My reading here is one that focuses on affect. Reading Philemon this way draws our attention to otherwise often hidden and emotional labor; it offers a moment for us to reflect on our present hyper-capitalist and interconnected service-economy world.

What will emerge (I hope) is not only a thorough, student-oriented review and overview of Philemon and its interpretive issues but also a meditation on the labor of interpretation itself. Interpretation is constructing meaning by not only the construction of contexts (both ancient and modern) and text but also the inter-animation between contexts and text. There is no singular, stable, fixed meaning "inside" a text. Meaning emerges also not strictly from within the reader. Instead, it is conjured out of the text through various types and levels of context and interpretive assumption used or generated by the reader.

Texts, all texts, are to some degree or another manuscripts randomly found in a library. Interpretations, all interpretations, involve a generative process, assembling meaning and sense out of pieces and fragments, building and rebuilding contexts, and arguments of coherence which assume a "plausible" or "probable" mantle from community consensus. Be admonished: of interpretation and reading, there is no end. Yet much more than a simple "weariness," the emerging intricate and powerful systems of web-like meaning-makings and significances are a joy to those attuned to them.

1

A Quick Overview of Paul's Letter to Philemon

As I mentioned in the Introduction, Philemon is among Paul's "undisputed" letters; almost all current scholarly interpretations affirm its authorship by Paul. Philemon is written in a dialect of ancient Greek known as "Koine" (meaning "common") or Hellenistic Greek. Ancient Greek is typically divided into three major periods: Epic or Homeric (also "Ionic"), which marks literature from the eighth century BCE; Classical or Attic Greek, which was the dialect used in imperial Athens and the language of the great tragedians and philosophers from the fifth and fourth century BCE; and Hellenistic or Koine Greek, which is the dialect that emerged after Alexander the Great conquered the Eastern Mediterranean world in the mid-fourth century BCE. Koine is marked by simple(r) grammatical structures, general wordiness and, for some, less nuance. It was the common language of industry, trade, travel, and commerce. In the Eastern provinces, even under Roman rule, Koine Greek was the standard language of local government. The Greek of the New Testament is notable for its generally lesser literary quality (e.g. when compared to the writings of Lucian, Plutarch, and other famous Greek writers of the first two centuries CE). Philemon, grammatically and rhetorically, is not much of an exception (though others have also found Philemon rhetorically complex enough to consider it "a gem"; see Bruce 1984; Church 1978; Jeal 2015).

There is no suggestion in the letter about the date of its composition, Paul's geographic location at the time of composition or even the location of Philemon's residence. Any information along these lines is external. Many scholars regard the canonical letter of Paul to the Colossians as pseudepigraphic, but Colossians refers to several characters who are also named in Philemon (more below). The earliest reference to (not quotation from)

Philemon is by the early Christian writer Tertullian (c. 155–c. 240 CE). The oldest extant fragment of Philemon contains most of vv. 13–15, 24–25; this papyrus (P87) dates from the late second to early third century (commonly dated 250 CE). Philemon makes no specific references to any datable events nor to any political or cultural figures which would assist us in dating the letter, though it does mention names common to several other first-century Christian documents, particularly to a cluster of documents associated with Paul and from what is now costal Turkey (especially the ancient city Colossae): Timothy, Epaphras, Mark, Demas, Aristarchus, and Luke (v. 24). There have never been challenges to the canonization or inclusion of Philemon within the New Testament, though it is omitted from some early lists (possibly because it was short, or because it was once circulated under the title "To the Laodiceans"). The letter claims Paul as its principal author (in collaboration with Timothy). Tradition unanimously suggests that Paul died sometime in the early to mid-60s CE. All the factors mentioned above would combine to suggest that Philemon was written sometime in the mid or the latter half of the first century CE. The Greek of Philemon—its vocabulary and grammar—is consistent with this dating.

Character and outline of Philemon

Philemon is the third shortest document in the New Testament, consisting of around 350 words in Greek (depending upon textual variations), all contained in one chapter of twenty-five verses or about nine to eleven sentences. It is approximately the length of one typed page of writing. Philemon is short for a letter attributed to Paul, since his other letters often span several chapters. In comparison with the rest of the New Testament, only 2 and 3 John are shorter than Philemon. Philemon is written primarily to one individual, though it imagines other readers: Philemon, Apphia, Archippus, and an entire house church are named as its recipients, but the bulk of the letter uses a second-person singular pronoun to refer to the addressee. Within the New Testament, only three other letters are similarly addressed to individuals (1 and 2 Timothy, Titus). Philemon's brevity and intimacy (i.e. it seems to be concerned with not problems of an entire community but a personal relationship) set it apart from Paul's other writings and from the bulk of the New Testament.

In the context of ancient letter writing, however, the letter to Philemon is far more conventional than other canonical New Testament epistles. Archaeologists have recovered a surprisingly large number of ancient letters (particularly given that most were written, as one would assume, on humble and readily decayable materials), and we also have extant a few ancient "style guides" or instructional essays for letter writing. In general, ancient letters were often short, to the (specific and singular) point and written to individuals (see Stower 1986). Letters in the early Roman Empire followed general formal conventions. They began with the name of the sender along with any titles, followed by the name(s) of the recipient(s). Philemon perfectly coheres to this norm. The letter then moves to a traditional greeting, often *charite* in Greek (which means "rejoice" or "greetings"). Paul adapts this convention with a play on words; he uses the word "*charis*" (grace). A letter would then (again, as does Philemon) "chat" very briefly with a blessing before turning to its major theme or request, which would make up the bulk of the letter. Ancient letters would occasionally conclude with pleasantries and more general greetings, including perhaps a petition to the gods for someone's health. Philemon also concludes with additional greetings from some of Paul's associates (and, presumably, common friends with Philemon) and a prayer.

Philemon can be outlined as follows:

I. Superscript: vv. 1–3.
    A. Senders and recipients, vv. 1–2
    B. General greeting, v. 3
II. Main Body: vv. 4–22.
    A. Paul's regard for Philemon, vv. 4–7
    B. Paul's request, vv. 8–20
        1. Preface: The state of Paul and Onesimus, vv. 8–11
        2. Paul is sending Onesimus back, despite Paul's desire to keep Onesimus near, vv. 12–14
        3. Paul's reflection on the estrangement/separation between Philemon and Onesimus, vv. 15–16
        4. Paul's hope for a good reunion and promise of support, vv. 17–18
        5. Paul's promise and reminder, vv. 19–20
            i.   A request "in his own hand"
            ii. An implied obligation from Philemon
    C. Paul's "confidence" and a second request, vv. 21–22
        1. "Confidence" in Philemon's obedience, v. 21
        2. Hopes for release and future travel (and request for lodgings), v. 22

> **III.** Concluding Greetings and Prayer: vv. 23–25.
>   **A.** Greetings from other common friends, vv. 23–24
>   **B.** Concluding prayer, v. 25

Ancient documents were handwritten. There was no mass reproduction, so multiple copies were also copied by hand. Of course, this process was both expensive and time consuming. It was also far from error-proof. In general, a manuscript would be better if it were copied by a professional scribe, but even professionals made errors. The most common errors are duplicate lines, skipped lines, misspellings, and other mistakes made when writing from memory. Occasionally, synonyms and homonyms creep into the document. Scholars spend years studying ancient languages and writing techniques; they then collect and compare all surviving copies of an ancient document. The process of analyzing these variations to reconstruct the most likely original reading is called "textual criticism."

The text of Philemon is considered relatively "stable." It has few significant or difficult variations; only a few cases where anything more untoward than a skipped or missing line or word in a surviving copy seem to have occurred. There are essentially seven notable manuscript variations—that is, places where several extant copies have different readings—in Philemon, and most of these are trivial. For example, in several manuscript copies Apphia is described as a "beloved" sister (in a few manuscripts, Apphia is even described as a "brother" despite the clearly feminine name). A slightly more difficult variation to resolve appears in v. 12 where some scribes seem to have inserted an extra word: *proslabou* ("you should take" or "you should receive"). The evidence as to what the original text contained is inconclusive. The most ancient manuscripts do not have the word "*proslabou*," though the sense of *proslabou* is clearly the sentence's intention. If a reader has trouble seeing any meaningful difference between these options, then my point is made; the variations in Philemon's text are generally not important or significant.

Philemon's most interesting textual variation is in v. 9. Paul pauses in or interrupts his entreaty with a statement of his own identity and his current situation (he will repeat *parakaleō*, "I entreat," in v. 10). This statement is a rhetorical appeal to pathos or a declaration of his status (or perhaps both), arising as if in reflex after his use of "I entreat" in v. 9. In the most commonly reconstructed Greek text, Paul describes himself as "an ambassador" (*presbutēs*) who is "now a prisoner." In some manuscripts, Paul describes himself as a *presbuteros*: an overseer, administrator, and, in later tradition, an elder or bishop. This variation is not difficult to resolve: the ancient manuscripts clearly point to *presbutēs*. *Presbutēs* has two senses in New Testament Greek (as well as in Koine Greek more generally). In the generic, it may refer to "an old man," but it also connotes "an elder" as in "a wise counselor," most likely complying with both the popular conceit that age begets wisdom and with the practicality that age often corresponds with career achievement and wealth accrual.

If we take *presbutēs* in its generic sense of "an old man," we have Paul making a pure appeal to pathos (i.e. the goodwill of his letter's recipient[s]): "I, Paul, an old man (and) now a prisoner." This would stress his appeal to Philemon in love rather than the more rigorous sense of a command (vv. 8–9). The letter to Philemon has no certain date, and we have no idea about the exact age of Paul when he wrote the letter. Tradition says that he died sometime in the mid-60s CE, and the Acts of the Apostles would suggest that Paul's incarceration(s), if we are to take "prisoner" literally, were in the latter half of his career. Paul would, then, reasonably be middle aged (though not likely "old"). Taking *presbutēs* as also an "ambassador" would imply that the modifier, "in or of Christ Jesus," may apply to both this term and the term "prisoner." If, however, we take *presbuteros* as the original reading, then we have a reading that (1) demonstrates a "downward trajectory" from "overseer" to "prisoner"; and (2) matches the dual pattern of vv. 8–9a, where authority is conjoined with love.

With basic issues such as author, date, and text of Philemon somewhat established, we can now turn to a quick review of Philemon's contents. In what follows, we'll focus on names or characters mentioned in Philemon and some "problem passages" found within the letter. Our examination of these topics will lay the groundwork for the discussions in later chapters.

The characters in Philemon

Paul and Timothy

The first word of the letter, as is customary in the canonical letters attributed to Paul, is "Paul." Paul frequently takes a title for himself in his letter greetings, yet in Philemon, his self-designation, "prisoner," is unique. In Romans (1.1), he describes himself as a "slave of Jesus Christ," a motif he repeats in Philippians. In 1 and 2 Corinthians as well as in Galatians, he self-designates as an apostle. In 1 and 2 Thessalonians, he takes no title. In the disputed epistles of Ephesians and Colossians, Paul is described as an apostle. In the Pastoral Letters, Paul is presented as both an apostle (1 and 2 Timothy and

Titus) and a slave (Tit. 1.1). The Pauline letters, as well as later, pseudo- or deutero-Pauline traditions, are rather consistent in terms of Paul's "self'-designations. Philemon is the only letter where Paul opens with the title "prisoner," even though references to incarceration also appear in Ephesians, Philippians, and Colossians. Indeed, the very word "prisoner" (*desmios*) is rare in Paul, appearing only here in v. 1 and again in v. 9 (though it also appears in letters that may not be genuinely written by Paul, such as Eph. 3.1 and 4.1 and 2 Tim. 1.8).

Philemon lists Timothy as Paul's coauthor and his brother. Designations of filial relationship are overwhelmingly metaphoric in Paul's writings, and particularly here in Philemon. In v. 10, Onesimus is referred to as Paul's "child" or "son," a relationship later, pseudo-Pauline traditions would ascribe also to Timothy (1 Tim. 1.2). Shortly on in Philemon, Paul will refer to Apphia as (his or Philemon's) "sister" (v. 2). Paul refers to multiple "family members" in Romans 16: Phoebe in 16.1; Andronicus and Junia in 16.7; Herodian in 16.11; Rufus and his mother in 16.13. Pauline writings often refer to fellow believers generically as "brethren" or "brothers." In general, then, it would be best to take familial designations as metaphoric and affective unless otherwise clarified; as we will see, this will be an important point for reading Philemon 16.

Timothy is a common associate of Paul in the New Testament literature, and he was particularly celebrated by later, pseudo-Pauline traditions. He is named as a coauthor of 2 Corinthians, Philippians, Colossians and 1 and 2 Thessalonians. Both Pauline and pseudo-Pauline traditions recognize the importance of Paul's association with Timothy. It is not precisely clear what coauthorship would entail: Timothy as a legitimate, second contributing author; Timothy as a scribe or secretary called an "amanuensis" (though Rom. 16.22 suggests that Paul does not consider his amanuensis for that letter, Tertius, a coauthor); or Timothy as the letter's delivery person. Philemon, as in all other cases in the Pauline literature, largely uses first-person singular verbs and pronouns to report individual reflections and reminiscences (e.g. Phlm 4). Once the letter proper begins, it reads as the voice of one person writing alone. According to Acts 16, Timothy (whose name in Greek means "lover of God") was a handpicked traveling companion, protégé, and fellow missionary of Paul. In Acts, he is often Paul's sole traveling companion. According to Acts 16.1, Timothy's mother, Eunice, was a Jew, while his father was a Gentile; Timothy was apparently reared with a general knowledge of Jewish Scripture and tradition, yet was not circumcised. The decision not to circumcise him as an infant would have been deliberate, and there are indications that such a choice was not unknown among diaspora Jews. In Acts

16.3, Paul for some reason—perhaps as a compromise?—requires Timothy to be circumcised. A later student of Paul's, intent on clarifying Paul's ideas about congregational governance, composed two letters to Timothy which were later canonized as 1 and 2 Timothy. Timothy is greeted at the conclusion of the letter to the Hebrews (Heb. 13.23); on the basis of this, many traditions have (erroneously) argued for Paul's authorship for Hebrews.

Philemon, Apphia, and Archippus

The letter is addressed, first, to Philemon. Most suggest, because of this, that Philemon is the letter's primary audience. The name "Philemon" means in Greek "lover of people" or "affectionate one." Based on a generic survey of inscriptional data, Philemon was not a common name from the first century, but it was also not particularly rare. No other mention of Philemon occurs within the canonical New Testament. He is referred to as "beloved" (*agapētos*), perhaps a play on words with his name. *Agapētos* could also be translated as "dear friend" (suggesting the Latin *amicus*). In Paul, *agapētos* is used with proper names (of individuals) here and in Rom. 16.8, 12; and as "dear friend" (clearly by sense or context) in Rom. 12.19; 1 Cor. 10.14; 2 Cor. 7.1; 12.19; Phil. 2.12. In Paul's letters, it is consistently used for close friends (but always within the context of addressing fellow believers in Jesus).

Philemon is also called a "fellow worker" (*sunergos*). The first-person plural pronoun "our" (the antecedent would be Paul and Timothy) is perhaps best applied to *sunergos*, though it might also apply to the earlier *agapētos*. In other words, either "Philemon, our dear friend and fellow worker" or "beloved Philemon, our fellow worker" are permissible translations. *Sunergos* in first-century Greek normally designates simply a "coworker" or fellow laborer (the general use also suggests physical labor). In Paul, it is most likely metaphoric and a very technical term. As witnessed in Rom. 16.3, 9, 21; Phil. 2.25; 4.3; 1 Cor. 16.16; 2 Cor. 6.1, the term most often designates individuals who have assisted Paul in spreading the word about Jesus as the Jewish Messiah. All of them (Paul, Timothy, and Philemon) would be fellow teachers or missionaries.

The second addressee is Apphia. She is unknown in the New Testament beyond this reference. In some manuscript variations she is referred to as "his sister." As earlier, we note that familial titles are most often metaphoric in Paul. Though Apphia may be Philemon's biological or legal sister, this would be incompatible with Paul's earlier reference to Timothy as his own brother. Shifting from a metaphoric use of "brother" to a literal sense of "sister" within one sentence seems awkward. "Sister" (*adelphē*) is also sometimes used for one's spouse in other Christian literature. The term is also used in patron-client relationships. The Greek text on which the Authorized Version (KJV) is based reads here not "sister" but "beloved."

Archippus is mentioned next. A person named Archippus is also mentioned in Col. 4.17. This is one of the principal reasons why some would consider Colossians to be genuinely written by Paul. As we will see, some twentieth-century scholars made much out of Archippus's mention in Colossians. Of course, many scholars today have reservations about Paul's authorship of Colossians (at minimum, that it may have been edited or altered from its original form). In this case, the mention of Archippus in Colossians only serves as evidence of an early date for Philemon's composition. Assertions that Archippus is the child of Philemon and Apphia, though as old as John Chrysostom, are pure imagination. Archippus is called "our fellow soldier" (*sustratiōtēs*). The term in normal first-century usage would denote a comrade in arms (particularly infantry). In early Christian literature the word is "used only figuratively of those who devote themselves to the service of the gospel; as a term of honor" (Danker et al. 2000: 979). *Sustratiōtēs* also appears in Phil. 2.25. The grammar and vocabulary of Philemon suggest that Archippus is a leader in the community.

The final recipients of the letter are "the church that meets in your [singular] house." The possessive pronoun's antecedent is unclear. Greek second-person pronouns will clarify number (singular or plural) but not gender, making it impossible to rule out any of the other three recipients as the owner of the home where the church assembly meets (and, thus, likely the main patron of the church assembly). One argument in favor of Apphia is that, as a woman, she would not normally be mentioned unless she was extremely prominent, perhaps the patron. This argument, however, assumes that women would not otherwise be prominent as teachers or leaders (unless they owned property). There is no basis for this assumption, particularly given the number of prominent women leaders mentioned in other letters by Paul (such as Romans 16). The other candidates are Philemon (who is the first person greeted and is the primary figure spoken to in the letter) or Archippus (who is the figure named in closest proximity to the singular pronoun "your"). The question cannot be resolved on the basis of grammar. It is also possible to suggest that Philemon and Apphia are married and members of a community that meets in Archippus's house.

In the first century, followers of Jesus met in small groups in private homes. Various house communities could certainly collaborate, and such might have been assumed in letters such as 1 Corinthians (where concerns of a larger, citywide community are being addressed, particularly divisions). The letter to Philemon does not seem to be addressed to a citywide community; we should probably imagine a small house community of a dozen to twenty fellow believers who met in a single home. At least two if not all three of the individuals named would be prominent members of that community; they were "coworkers" (teachers or missionaries), "fellow soldiers" and close associates of Paul and Timothy.

Onesimus

Onesimus is named in v. 10, and this is the only time his name occurs in the letter despite the fact that he seems to be the reason for it. The sequence of clauses describing Onesimus moves him in an opposite direction from Paul. While Paul's life trajectory has been one that moved from authority ("ambassador") to debasement ("prisoner"), Onesimus has gained in status, at least in Paul's assessment of the world.

Much seems to have changed (recently?) for Onesimus. Paul devotes three parallel clauses in vv. 10–13 to express his perspective on Onesimus. Onesimus is the one whom Paul is sending back (to Philemon), the one who is Paul's own heart, who is Philemon's "brother" and the one whom Paul would have been glad to keep as companion to serve Paul in Philemon's stead. It is clear that Paul has a relationship in faith and love with Onesimus and a relationship in faith and love with Philemon; what Paul seeks now is for Onesimus and Philemon to be united in mutual service and love as well. All three characters are to be united by affection, service, and need as well as interlacing love, word, and duty. The interconnections among the three characters should involve acts of affective and effective mercy. As we will see, the central themes to emerge in this letter are authority and friendship, patronage and service, command and love, usefulness and confinement, reunion and separation.

Onesimus is the fifth person named so far (excluding Paul), but he is clearly the focus of Paul's energy. The name "Onesimus" was not uncommon. It translates roughly as "handy" or "useful." It was a particularly common name for a slave. In the Greco-Roman world, slavery was rampant. It encompassed nearly all skilled, semi-skilled, and unskilled labor. The majority of the population was likely enslaved. Verse 16 suggests to some that

Onesimus was (at least at one time) a slave. Historically, Christian exegesis of Philemon has argued that Onesimus was not only a slave but also a fugitive slave. None of this is explicit in the letter (particularly the suggestion of a fugitive), though it is certainly a possible reading. We will discuss slavery and its relevance to the interpretation of Paul's letter to Philemon at much greater length in later chapters.

The name "Onesimus" appears also in Col. 4.9. Colossians has a deep affinity with Ephesians (portions of these letters are verbatim); as a result, Colossians, Ephesians, and Philemon are frequently grouped together as the "prison epistles." The repetitions, along with some other thematic elements (notably a sense of Jesus as a pre-incarnate Christ figure) in Colossians and Ephesians, seem to not only set these letters apart from Paul's other writings but also reflect circumstances and theological concerns that arose after Paul's death. Many, then, see Colossians and Ephesians as pseudepigraphic. Strangely, however, even though many note the resonances among Colossians, Ephesians, and Philemon, current scholarship tends not to challenge the Pauline authorship of Philemon. Instead, these resonances (such as references in Colossians to characters in Philemon, like Archippus and Onesimus) suggest only an attempt of mimicry intended to authenticate a pseudo-Pauline letter as genuinely by Paul.

According to later Christian literature, an Onesimus was named as the bishop of the congregation(s) in Ephesus (Ignatius, *Eph.* 1.3; 2.1; 6.2). Indeed, an ancient (secular) inscription from Ephesus also lists a prominent individual in the city named Onesimus (*CIG* 2983). Christian tradition since Chrysostom has argued that Onesimus, a fugitive slave of Philemon converted by Paul, was returned to Philemon along with this letter (see Chapter 3 in this volume). Philemon received Onesimus back, set him free, and, in time, Onesimus became a leader in the early church, rising to the status of being the bishop of Ephesus. Some scholars have even suggested that Onesimus was the individual responsible for the preservation and collection of Paul's letters as a corpus. All of this, of course, is raw conjecture based on scattered data and terms. As we will see, the ancient tradition behind this narrative is uniform, though it is also late, and there are questionable assumptions of continuity that underlie it.

As I have already mentioned, Onesimus's name appears only once in Paul's letter to Philemon (v. 10), despite Onesimus's circumstances being the occasion and reason for the letter's existence. One might note, somewhat cynically, that Paul's own name appears three times. Furthermore, Onesimus, when described, is generally defined by what he is *to Paul* (e.g. useful, a good servant, very dear, a "begotten son") or to Philemon (no longer a slave but a brother);

very little—well, more precisely, nothing at all—is said about Onesimus himself as a person. We learn nothing of what Onesimus feels and desires. Onesimus is only the second-most interesting (at best) or even the third-most interesting figure in the letter. He, useful or not, effective or not, slave or not, is mostly invisible in this letter; he is seen entirely in the light of Paul's own interests and desire(s) as well as Philemon's obligations and authority.

Verse 11 has another of Paul's play on words (cf. *charis* and *agapētos* in v. 1, as mentioned above), and his most elaborate one. As we noted earlier, the name Onesimus could be roughly translated as "handy" or "useful." Making a play on the name, Paul describes Onesimus as "formerly useless." There is very likely a double pun here. The word in Greek is *achrēston*, which does not appear elsewhere in Paul's letters (let alone in the rest of the New Testament). It has the negating prefix "a-" (so "not," "without," or "un-") attached to the word for "use" (*chrēstos*). One can readily see the similarity between this word and the Greek *christos* or "anointed," which, of course, is the term applied to Jesus as the Messiah ("Christ"). Formerly, Onesimus ("Handyman") was "useless" (*achrēston*) when he was without faith in Jesus as Christ (*a-christos*, so to speak). This wordplay continues with Paul's assertion that Onesimus is now "useful" (*euchrēstos*). Here, the prefix "eu-" ("well," "suitable," or "proper") is attached to *chrēstos*. Onesimus is now "useful" (literally, "well-used"), because he has been "well-christed." More darkly, *euchrēstos* occurs in many bawdy references in contemporary literature; to be "useful" was to be sexually available. We will discuss this further in Chapter 2, but let it suffice to note now that many slaves in antiquity were "useful" sexually to their masters (Marchal 2011). One justifiably wonders how a slave named Onesimus, a name that is not really a name, would regard a "clever" wordplay at his expense. Even at its best, Onesimus was "useless" before he came to believe in the messianic status of Jesus. Now a believer in Jesus and a servant to Paul, Onesimus has become "useful." Onesimus has moved from servile slave to (still servile) believer, from uselessness to usefulness (to others). While Onesimus has hence elevated in status, his worth is still defined by his ability to be of service. Though this may seem pejorative to suggest about a fellow follower of Jesus (at the minimum, callous to point out in his presence), the emphasis on productivity is an equation that is consistent with Paul's general human calculus. Philemon's love is praised by Paul because it is effectual, productive, or useful; Philemon's *agapē* leads him to action. Similarly, Paul assesses his own state in terms of his ability to proclaim or reveal his message about Jesus; he may be a prisoner, but he is still a productive "coworker" for Christ.

The letter hints that Onesimus and Philemon are estranged. Verse 15 is the first of two conciliatory views on the separation between Onesimus and Philemon. Paul is going to argue that the estrangement served a purpose, with subtle hints that this was possibly providential. "Perhaps for this" hints at God's action (and perhaps also an allusion to Est. 4.14, though the significance of such an allusion is unclear). All verbs in the clause are passive; no one is viewed as being the cause for the estrangement or being blamed for the separation. Paul also contrasts the short separation, "a little while" (ōran; literally, "an hour"), with the lengthy restoration that will be "forever" (aiōnion; literally, "an age" or "an eon").

We encounter in v. 18 not only the second conciliatory view on the separation between Onesimus and Philemon but also another locus for arguments that Onesimus was a fugitive slave. Such readings argue that the source of damages (which seem to be financial) are costs incurred by Onesimus's escape. This need not be the case, however. Paul, with a conditional sentence, is saying that if Onesimus has "done you any wrong" (adikeō), Paul himself will somehow make it good. Adikeō is literally "unjust," "unfair," "inappropriate," or "unfit." It is the negation of dikē, which has been translated in English as "righteousness" since the Authorized Version (KJV). Such translation suggests to modern English speakers a moral transgression. Indeed, a moral lapse is certainly one way to understand adikeō. Yet the translation also masks for modern English speakers the broader range of usage for this term, as it may simply mean "unfit," "unfair," or "inappropriate." Greek use of adikeō describes offenses that include moral violations (e.g. murder, rape, adultery), legal and economic violations, or, simply, breaches of etiquette or decorum. In Paul's use, it tends to connote "doing wrong," though also with a varied range of severity (1 Cor. 6.7, 8; 2 Cor. 7.2, 12; Gal. 4.12). Other uses in the New Testament suggest more simply "causing damage" (Rev. 7.2; 9.4, 10). This latter sense can include financial damage or loss, of course. The thought that Paul is imagining financial damages, as opposed to simply moral or ethical pain, is reinforced by his use of "credit" (elloga) and the clause "he owes anything at all" (opheilei), both of which have a much stronger economic connotation. Verse 19 clearly implies economic remuneration.

Paul is asking that the damages or debts (moral and economic) caused by the estrangement be placed upon Paul's own shoulders. One wonders, though, what financial assets Paul has to make good on this offer. Perhaps, Paul is counting on Philemon negating any debts, both because Paul did not himself incur them and because of Philemon's prior relationship with Paul.

Paul's not-too-subtle reminder to Philemon of Philemon's own indebtedness to Paul would reinforce this idea. Paul himself might also be the source of estrangement between Onesimus and Philemon.

Luke, Mark, Aristarchus, Demas, and Epaphras

These are quite minor characters in Philemon, being mentioned only in the closing remarks (v. 23), but they are significant to many interpreters who use other books in the canonical New Testament to piece together Paul's travels and biography. Verse 23's mention of Epaphras is a critical datum for many seeking to locate the place and time of Paul's writing of this letter. The letter to Colossae also mentions Epaphras (a common name and the diminutive of the name, Epaphroditus) as the founder of the Colossian church (Col. 1.7; 4.12), in addition to the note that Paul is in prison (Col. 4.10). In Phlm 23 Epaphras is described as Paul's "fellow prisoner" (*sunaichmalōtos*; cf. Rom. 16.7; Col. 4.10), which also set him apart from the list of names to follow (as he is the only one being designated as "fellow prisoner" in this letter), though the root word Paul uses here is different from the one he uses for his own self-designation as "prisoner" earlier in v. 1 and v. 9. The particular role being given to Epaphras in Colossians and in Philemon suggests to some that Philemon and the church assembly with him reside in or near Colossae. The extension of third-party greetings by Paul is a typical means Paul uses to close his letters (cf. Rom. 16.3, 5–16; 1 Cor. 16.19–20; 2 Cor. 13.12; Phil. 4.21–22; [Col. 4.10–17]; 1 Thess. 5.26) and is imitated in the pseudo-Pauline letters as well (2 Tim. 4.19, 21; Tit. 3.15).

The list of third-party greetings continues in v. 24 with four more names. Two (Aristarchus and Demas) are fairly minor figures, but the other two (Mark and Luke) are major figures in the New Testament and in the history of Christianity. All four are described as "fellow workers" (a title also used for Philemon in v. 1 above). Taking the minor characters first, Aristarchus is a character mentioned also in Acts (19.29; 20.4; 27.2) and in Colossians (4.10). Again, we have parallels or echoes between Colossians and Philemon. According to Acts, Aristarchus travels with Paul during Paul's collection program for the poor in Jerusalem, and Paul's distribution of those monies is his last act as a free man; following this event, Paul is incarcerated. Demas, short for Demetrios, is mentioned in Col. 4.14 and 2 Tim. 4.10. Nothing else is known of him.

Greetings are extended also from Mark. This figure seems to be the same individual who is mentioned as the son of Mary of Jerusalem (Acts 12.12). He is said to be a cousin of Barnabas (Col. 4.10), who also introduced Mark to Paul (Danker et al. 2000: 617). In Acts, Mark travels with Paul on Paul's first missionary journey, yet leaves and returns home; Barnabas then has a disagreement with Paul about whether or not to take Mark on a second journey (Acts 12.12, 25; 15.37, 39). Paul and Barnabas, as a result, separate (apparently permanently as a missionary partnership); Barnabas takes Mark while Paul takes Timothy as his protégé. No reunion between Paul and Barnabas is ever described in Acts. If this is the same figure, apparently Mark is now again working with Paul (and, recalling v. 1, also with Timothy). Mark is mentioned again in both a pseudo-Pauline (2 Tim. 4.11) and a non-Pauline letter (1 Pet. 5.13). According to the fourth-century historian Eusebius of Caesarea, Mark later became a companion of Peter, serving as his interpreter during Peter's incarceration. Eusebius also claims that Mark wrote down Peter's memoirs into a single document, which tradition identifies as the Gospel of Mark.

Luke is often named as Paul's companion in Paul's later years, including Paul's most extensive incarceration and his final journey to Rome. Luke is mentioned also in Col. 4.14 and 2 Tim. 4.11. Colossians indicates that Luke is Paul's physician (though this has been disputed by scholars). Traditional scholarship, drawing upon these references and the use of "we" in later chapters of Acts that describe Paul's travels, argues that Luke is the author of both the Gospel of Luke and of the Acts of the Apostles.

It may be important to note that all four figures named by Paul in this conclusion—and seven of the nine characters named in Philemon—are also named in Colossians.

Philemon's trouble spots

Even though the letter is rather short, there are still a few places in Philemon where the letter is very unclear and could generate extensive interpretive debates.

Whose church assembly?

One question arises from the very beginning. Paul includes among his addresses "and the church that meets in your (sing.) house," leaving room for debate as to whose house, and what church, he intends. The Greek word for "assembly" (*ekklēsia*) is commonly anachronistically translated as "church." In Classical and Koine Greek, *ekklēsia* is a political term meaning "summoned assembly." It is the common word for trials, voting assemblies, and other deliberative and legislative bodies. Other terms for the early congregations of Jesus followers are similarly political. For example, Matthew's "kingdom" (*basileia*) of God is the same Greek term that the Roman Empire used to designate itself. Ancient followers of Jesus saw themselves as creating an alternative political community. *Ekklēsia* as a general gathering of people is not unknown in the New Testament (e.g. Acts 19.32, 40). The word is also used for a congregation of Jews (e.g. Acts 7.38), so it also suggests an alternative political identity (through which Jews saw themselves as an ethnicity or a community different from the Roman imperial norm). Jews of the late Second Temple period might well also have understood themselves as summoned by God to be a people set apart from others (as descendants of Abraham and entrusted with the Torah). Paul readily adopts this term for his assemblies of Jesus followers.

While "assembly" or "church" may be clear enough, what remains a mystery is the antecedent of "your" in "your home." The three possibilities are, of course, Philemon, Apphia or Archippus. In defense of Philemon, his name is mentioned first in the sequence. Of course, this may also be because he is the principal addressee. Archippus has also been suggested as the assembly leader, largely on the basis of his appearance in Colossians and that his name is closest in the sentence to "your home." Of course, if Colossians is pseudo-Pauline, this reference would be arising from Philemon, not confirming his importance in Philemon. Another strong possibility is Apphia, since it would otherwise be unusual for Paul to mention a woman by name. In the other places where Paul does name a woman, she is clearly a leader (Phoebe in Rom. 16.1–2; Junia in Rom. 16:7; and Chloe in 1 Cor. 1.11); at the very least, the leadership of the named female is strongly implied (Euodia and Syntyche in Phil. 4.2–3).

Why this roundabout rhetoric?

A second perplexing aspect of Philemon is Paul's complicated series of denials and obfuscations. Paul repeatedly, and somewhat confusedly, asserts that he has the right to command Philemon (v. 8) but is eschewing that right (vv. 9, 11, 14), only to claim also that Philemon owes Paul Philemon's very life (v. 19) and that he is "confident of" Philemon's "obedience" (v. 21). Is Paul commanding Philemon or just asking for a favor? If he really doesn't want to intimidate or command, why does Paul stress his authority so much? If he feels that he actually has the authority (actual and moral) that he seems to suggest he has, why doesn't Paul come right out and insist upon his request?

One gets the sense that there is too much protest in Paul's rhetoric. There is inherent rhetorical effect (and threat) in saying, "I could simply compel you." A reminder of one's authority, even when followed by a statement to abdicate that authority, still has an effect of intimidation. Notice the tone and effect of v. 14 and v. 19. There are two ways, then, of reading this preamble: either Paul is subtly pressuring Philemon to do what Paul wants or Paul is genuinely asking Philemon for help. Much depends upon how one regards Paul's general character.

The word "command" (*epitassein*) in v. 8 does not appear elsewhere in Paul's writings. It does occur in Mk. 9.25. There, as in other Koine Greek usage, the term suggests a barked order. It is a fitting term to use in v. 8 alongside "duty" (*anēkon*), another rare word in the Pauline literature (it occurs elsewhere only in Col. 3.18 and Eph. 5.4, both letters with debated authorship). It suggests what is "fitting" or "proper." In summary, then, Paul opens by stressing that he has the authority, through his relationship to Christ, to order Philemon (aggressively) to, in effect, "snap to" his duty. Certainly, these are odd words to select as openings to a request that is fully optional. Despite what follows in v. 9, it seems very unlikely that Paul's preamble to his request here is designed to assuage Philemon's (real or imagined) sense of obligation.

A more likely translation of vv. 8–9a is: "Even though I am confident enough through Christ to order you, I also entreat you out of love." It becomes critical to decide if the sense is "I also entreat you" or "instead, I entreat you" (RSV). In the RSV's (protective?) translation of these verses, Paul is deferring his authority to command because of his preference to appeal to affection. But a better reading of the Greek in Philemon suggests that Paul is *adding* an appeal to affection to his command to duty, since the comparative adjective "more" (*mallon*) in v. 9 parallels the more minimal "enough" (*pollēn*) that modifies Paul's confidence in v. 8. Both translations, however, do communicate that Paul wants to inspire not only actual but also affectual compliance. Paul wants his request honored, and he wants Philemon to want to comply. This parallels his command to give alms "not out of necessity" in 2 Cor. 9.6–11.

It is not entirely clear whether Paul is suggesting that his request should place Philemon in a moral or personal sense of obligation, or whether Paul is asserting that he could actually override Philemon's authority. Paul is clearly assuming that Philemon does possess some responsibility for or authority over Onesimus. This may indicate Philemon's ownership of Onesimus. It may also suggest that Onesimus belongs to Philemon's household (and, as we noted earlier, there are a variety of possible reasons for this, including Onesimus's status as a minor). If Philemon possesses legal (and economic) authority over Onesimus, Paul cannot legally or automatically overrule this authority, despite Paul's intimation otherwise. Only very highly placed government officials could do such things. Paul is almost certainly referencing his authority "in Christ," an authority that he may feel would overrule Philemon's use of legal recourse. The Roman government would, of course, see it otherwise. Paul may also be aware that if he acted at his own discretion, Philemon, because of his affectionate bond with or respect for Paul, would be personally or psychologically compelled to concede. Whatever the case, Paul says that he did not want to act without Philemon's "knowledge" (*gnōmēs*) or "consent" (v. 14). Suspicious readers could well ask if Philemon would grant Paul this presumed authority. Perhaps Paul is "spinning" a situation in which he does not have the actual authority (moral or otherwise) to act.

Paul reminds Philemon of Philemon's own debt to him (v. 19). Paul indicates that he "need not say" Philemon is indebted to him. Of course, if one really "need not say" something, one doesn't. Paul is clearly invoking the specter of Philemon's debt as a rhetorical means of persuading Philemon to absolve Onesimus's debt. Philemon is now in a situation of limited choices. He may (1) ignore Paul (to whom he is indebted) and require remittance from Onesimus (which denies a depth of relationship he has with Paul); (2) assign Onesimus's debt to Paul, to whom Philemon is indebted, and appear rather callous; or (3) simply absorb the losses quietly. Philemon's debt to Paul is "his very life'—literally, "you owe me your very self" (v. 19c).

Paul also reminds Philemon that debts are not only of the past, but remain in the present. They are always unremitted, perhaps even unremittable. Paul makes this clear in v. 19 by his use of "owing" (*prosopheileis*), which clearly suggests a debt still owed (Danker et al. 2000: 883–84). This is the only time this word occurs in Paul's letters (indeed, in the entire New Testament). The sense is that Philemon, if demanding repayment, is ungracious in a way that others (namely, Paul) have not been to him. Of course, this reminds the New Testament reader of Jesus's parable of the "ungrateful steward" (Mt. 18.21–35).

Reminding Philemon that his very life is (still) indebted to Paul may suggest an even more audacious claim. Slavery in the Roman world, unlike slavery in antebellum America, was largely an economic relationship (rather than ethnic or racial). Slaves, in many circumstances, became slaves because of economic need. Indebted and without means to repay, individuals sold or bartered themselves (or, in dire cases, family members) in exchange for debt. Further, slaves, even those from birth, were occasionally allowed opportunity to amass funds to purchase their own freedom. Slave ownership erased individual identities. Indeed, slaves could be pejoratively referred to as "bodies" or "(living) things" (Glancy 2006). Absolution of debt in Paul is both a spiritual and a flatly economic problem.

Read alongside v. 16, Paul may be "asking" Philemon in vv. 17–21 to either allow Paul to purchase Onesimus's freedom, to take Paul in Onesimus's stead or to set Onesimus free. If this were the case, then these verses would be the emotional center of the entire epistle. Yet, if the request to manumit Onesimus is Paul's real focus, he's being very coy and oblique about a matter Onesimus, for one, would want to be made very clear. Paul is not elsewhere coy about telling people what to do with very personal and domestic matters, including manumission from slavery (1 Cor. 7.1–40). He is, however, sometimes oblique about requests for money or support (Rom. 15.23–29). Though this is admittedly conjecture, it seems more in character with Paul, at least in my view, that he is asking Philemon for Onesimus's return to serve Paul than for Onesimus's manumission (though, I'm sure, the ideal would be for both outcomes to occur).

While the meaning of "receiving back" is debatable, "receiving back" Onesimus is certainly the letter's main theme. The "central nervous system" of Philemon's body, or the skeleton from which all other thoughts hang, is "I, Paul, entreat you concerning Onesimus." As I have mentioned, this thought is prefaced carefully and "I entreat" is repeated (vv. 9, 10). Paul asserts his authority to command Philemon, but clarifies that he is also—instead?— making an appeal rooted in love (vv. 8–9). After expressing his entreaty, Paul quickly employs the language of familial intimacy, albeit in a way which preserves Paul's dominant status: he is father to Onesimus (v. 10). Later remarks in the letter suggest that Philemon, like Onesimus, was a beneficiary of Paul (v. 19). This parallel in their respective relationship to Paul would quietly suggest that Onesimus and Philemon are equals.

Precisely why Philemon is so carefully and delicately arranged, however, is anything but clear. Paul may be worried that his "request" will be interpreted as a command, whether intentional or implied (vv. 8–10). He may also be concerned that his request is bordering on improper or offensive. He may realize his request operates on a logic that is not prima facie obvious. It's hard, at least for me, to imagine the author of Corinthians, Galatians, and Romans as being overly concerned with propriety, offense, or appearing authoritarian. The subsequent (and simpler) clause may also be the central request: that Onesimus be allowed to remain with Paul (v. 13a). If so, the remarks about how Paul has grown so fond of Onesimus and how Onesimus has served Paul in Philemon's absence have laid the foundation for Paul's appeal and its persuasion. Paul is stressing his own distressed condition, his personal affection for Onesimus, and a desire that Philemon respond to Onesimus's return in ways that Paul sees as warm. The anacoluthon betrays either Paul's own ambivalence about Onesimus leaving or his concern about how Philemon will receive Onesimus, or both.

What does Paul really want?

A third question in Philemon is: What *is* Paul's request precisely? Paul "entreats" (*parakaleō*) Philemon, finally getting to the purpose of the letter after nearly a third of the way into its composition. Even after this delay, Paul does not come quickly to the content of his entreaty. He will first describe his current state in v. 9 (before repeating *parakaleō* again in v. 10). *Parakaleō* is frequent in Paul and is used in nearly every sense that the word is used in Koine Greek. By far, the most common sense in Paul is "urge," "exhort," or "encourage" (Rom. 12.1, 8; 15.30; 16.17; 1 Cor. 1.10; 4.16; 14.31; 16.15; 2 Cor. 2.8; 6.1; 8.6; 10.1; Phil. 4.2; 1 Thess. 2.12; 4.1; 5.11, 14). The word also suggests "comfort," which is yet again a usage found frequently in Paul (Rom. 12.8; 2 Cor. 1.4, 6; 2.7; 7.6, 7, 13; 13.11; 1 Thess. 3.2, 7; 4.18). Rarely, however, does Paul use the word to mean "request" or "implore"; indeed, he does so only here and in 1 Cor. 16.12 and 2 Cor. 9.5.

In v. 10, Paul returns to his appeal (repeating *parakaleō*). He is writing on behalf of someone very dear to himself. "Begat" (*egennēsa*) refers to childbirth. The metaphor is that Paul has "given birth" to Onesimus in guiding him to follow Jesus. Paul uses birth metaphors for following Jesus (Galatians 4) and "new life" as a description of living as a Jesus follower (Romans 5). "My child" or "my son" (the masculine singular form of "child" is used, so either translation is strictly correct) is no doubt metaphoric; Onesimus is not Paul's literal son any more than he was literally "begotten" or "given birth" by Paul. As mentioned earlier, Paul nearly always uses familial terms metaphorically. Paul again uses the term "prisoner" to describe himself in v. 10. This entire verse is filled with words designed to appeal to affect and pathos.

Paul also asks for "some benefit" (*onaimēn*) from Philemon in v. 20. *Onaimēn* occurs only here in the New Testament, though it appears in later Christian writings, notably the letters of the second-century martyr Ignatius (*Pol.* 6.2; *Magn.* 12.2). The use of the word here also parallels Paul's request for

Roman (financial) support in Romans 15. It may be translated as "have bene-fit," "receive," "have for use," or "enjoy." In other words, it is a part of Paul's style to use roundabout rhetoric when he is asking for money or material support.

The obvious substance of Paul's request, given the letter so far, would be Onesimus's return for his own "use." This would account for his repeated language about Onesimus's usefulness to himself and service in Philemon's stead. It clearly suggests that Paul would find Philemon's removal of Onesimus's "debt" (either by simply forgiving it or by imput-ing it to Paul) as a "benefit." At minimum, it suggests (perhaps meta-phorically?) that Paul would consider taking Onesimus's debt as the "enjoyment" of Philemon's property. The letter seems to link emotion, faith, and labor together.

For example, as we have just seen in v. 20, Paul calls for Philemon to "refresh my heart in Christ." "Refresh" (*anapauson*), also in v. 7 above, may imply "give ease from labor." "Heart" is *splagchna*. It refers to the seat of one's emotions, but Paul has also used it ("my own heart") as a metaphor for Onesimus in v. 12. Oddly, "heart" occurs in this epistle more often than the names "Philemon" and "Onesimus" combined. To "refresh Paul's heart" could simply mean that Philemon's reception of Onesimus without demand-ing Onesimus's debts (moral or actual) would encourage Paul. To "refresh Paul's heart," with the suggestion of "release from labor or obligation," could mean to forgive Onesimus's debt (which Paul has asked be made his own). It may be a request that Onesimus, still a slave or not, be returned to Paul to labor with Paul and for Paul's needs. It may mean Paul is asking that his "heart" (i.e. Onesimus) be "released from labor" (i.e. set free). In this latter reading, the return to hierarchical language in v. 20 ("in lordship" and "in Christ"), particularly when used so closely on the heels of language about debt (particularly Philemon's outstanding debt of his very life to Paul), would be a subtle reminder to Philemon that he himself had been "set free" by God and God's authority, which is represented by Paul who is now a "prisoner" of Christ. It would also continue the motif of and stress on slavery. This mixture of emotion, faith, and labor (or slavery?) does not, however, clarify Paul's precise request of Philemon, especially given the enigmatic v. 21 that Paul expects Philemon to do "even more."

Who is the real center?

As I have mentioned briefly above, Onesimus is evaluated principally by his relationship (or potential relationship) to Paul. In v. 9, Paul interrupts his entreaty by restating his identity (creating an emphasis rhetorically on himself). In v. 11, Paul again stresses himself by the use of the first-person pronoun (*egō*). Paul will use *egō* three more times in this letter (vv. 19 [twice], 20). This would be a highly unusual number of uses for such a short letter. He also repeats his own name twice (vv. 9, 19) and stresses that he is writing with his own hand (v. 19). The effect is something like "I, Paul, me, I'm writing to ask something." Clearly, Paul is interested in stressing his own voice. The reason why, however, is unclear. Suggestions may include (1) Paul is appealing to his own authority or reputation; (2) Paul is playing on Philemon's affections; or (3) Paul is clarifying his ideas or preferences from some other reports or rumors.

Paul's attention in this letter is remarkably self-centered. Onesimus, as we are seeing, is constantly defined and identified vis-à-vis others (either Paul's love for him or his own estrangement from Philemon). His only independent attribute is "usefulness" to others. Of about 350 words in Paul's letter to Philemon, 42 are either first-person pronouns, first-person verbs or Paul's own name. I do not count words that refer to Paul (e.g. "prisoner," "slave," "old man"). More than one in six words in Philemon, perhaps as many as one in five, refer to Paul himself.

Verse 13 again calls attention to Paul. The phrase there, "so that he might serve me on your behalf" (*hina huper sou moi diakonē*), begins with the particle *hina*, a rather straightforward particle indicating that what comes next expresses the purpose of the preceding clause or verb. It may normally be translated as "so that," "in order that" or "as a result." What follows will be the reason why Paul would desire Onesimus to remain in his company. Note, by the way, that Paul's interest is not Onesimus's basic character and company, but, once again, his usefulness.

The word "service" (*diakonē*) is significant. The word, in general Koine Greek, is one associated with slavery or compulsory service. It may be contrasted with *doulos*, which normally suggests physical, arduous labor. In general, *diakonē* connotes "attendance upon," so some lighter, perhaps domestic or administrative, tasks. Within the New Testament, *diakonos* (the nominal form) is frequently employed for service or "ministry" to others, perhaps with a particular focus on attending to another's physical needs, such as in the administration of charity and the distribution of alms (so Acts 6). In 1 Timothy and Titus, it appears to connote a set ecclesiastical office. It also applies to the central "table service" of Christian devotion: namely, the administration of the elements of the Christian ritual meal (the Lord's Supper, as it is called in 1 Corinthians). Paul refers to himself and other coworkers as "deacons" (using a form of *diakonia*, though it is normally translated in English as "servants" or "ministers"). Paul's use here could relate to personal service, something similar to the tasks being performed today by a secretary, valet, butler, and so on. These would certainly be involved in the meaning of *diakonē*. Paul does not seem to be imagining an official church office that Onesimus will perform; there is also little to indicate that Paul is thinking of liturgical activity.

Verse 14 seems to repeat the desire Paul just expressed for Onesimus to remain and serve Paul while Paul is in prison. Paul is entreating Philemon on Onesimus's behalf, but would be happy to have Philemon send Onesimus back in turn. This verse ends the elaborate sentence that began in v. 8, suggesting that it is the culmination of Paul's entreaty. Paul has noted Onesimus's change in becoming a Jesus follower, including his usefulness in general and his usefulness to Paul in particular. In addition to emphasizing Onesimus's service to Paul (in Philemon's place), Paul also features his own work with and affection for Onesimus. Paul is now hinting in v. 14 that he, though tempted to keep Onesimus nearby, wants to give Philemon the chance to respond out of "his own will." In other words, the flow of the letter goes from Paul explaining Onesimus's utility (particularly to Paul) to Paul expressing his desire to retain Onesimus. Philemon's treatment or reception of Onesimus may be the major concern of this letter, but Paul himself seems to occupy the letter's central space.

When Paul makes a point to repeat his own name in v. 19 to clarify that his own hand (i.e. his own signature) undergirds the request and the promise to "repay," Paul is in essence providing credibility that the claim for remittance comes from him as well as something like an informal promissory note. For the third time in this letter, Paul both uses the first-person singular pronoun and repeats his name (vv. 1, 9, 19). To make the latter point more dramatic, we might observe that Onesimus's name occurs only once (v. 10), as does Philemon's (v. 1). Paul uses his own name more than the other two principal names combined. Whatever the status of Onesimus and Philemon or the relationship between them may be, the most important and central figure in the intercessory letter of Paul to Philemon remains Paul. His name begins and seals the document, just as his interests and desire permeate its body.

How are they related?

Perhaps the most acute debate in Philemon is the relationship between Onesimus and Philemon. As we will see, the leading options are: (1) Onesimus is a slave owned by Philemon; (2) Onesimus and Philemon have no relationship—Onesimus is the slave of Archippus (this idea is limited to one somewhat eclectic school of readers in the twentieth century); (3) Onesimus and Philemon are estranged brothers. Most of these debates surround how one reads the complex sentence in v. 16.

Having reinterpreted the duration of the estrangement between Onesimus and Philemon in v. 15 ("for a while"), Paul turns in v. 16 to the nature of their relationship and its transformation as a result of recent events. Onesimus is now returned to Philemon "no longer as a slave" but as a "beloved brother," suggesting at minimum that the estrangement's severity or loss has been mitigated, remedied or compensated. In American biblical interpretation, this verse has historically been the center of criticism and commentary on Philemon (Harrill 2000). This verse was the center of nineteenth-century debates over slavery. One could read this verse (as do traditional Christian exegetes) as finally clarifying that Onesimus was Philemon's slave. Suddenly, the references and allusions to Philemon's authority over Onesimus, Onesimus's unusual name, Paul's reticent rhetoric and the attention to Onesimus's "usefulness" all make sense. Paul is stressing that Onesimus is now not (just) a slave, but a believer and a "brother"; Philemon is now in the suddenly delicate position of owning another believer in Jesus who is also a (fugitive?) slave, and Paul is trying to help negotiate this tension. Traditional American exegesis of the nineteenth century generally embraced exactly this reading. Some went on to observe that Paul was sending the slave Onesimus back and argued that this offered moral authority to fugitive slave laws and proved the Bible's endorsement of slavery. Paul does not compel Philemon to free Onesimus, even though the latter is a Christian.

The identification of Onesimus as a slave is certainly possible. Paul uses the Greek *doulos*, which is the strongest of possible words for "slave." Paul asserts that Onesimus is taken back no longer (just) as a *doulos*, but even more than a *doulos*. Yet, Paul also asserts that Philemon and Onesimus are brothers (*adelphos*). The debate becomes: Are the words "slave" and "brother" metaphoric? Both? Which? Neither? As we have seen, Paul uses both slave and familial language metaphorically in his letters; Paul calls himself a "slave of Jesus Christ" in Rom. 1.1, and he presents Timothy as his "brother" in Philemon 1. Indeed, Paul uses such language metaphorically so frequently that one should generally assume that the usage is metaphoric unless there is clear indication from context that one should not. Frustratingly, we almost have exactly such an indication in this sentence. The critical words, however, are "almost … exactly." Were the language here *either* more precise *or* more ambivalent the question would be less difficult.

At the center of the issue is the phrase, "both in flesh [or 'according to the flesh' or 'fleshly'] and in the lord [again, 'according to the lord' or 'lordly']" (*kai en sarki kai en kuriō*). The definite article is not present in the Greek; the language is literally "in flesh" and "in lord." Is "in flesh and in lord" adverbial (so "he's physically and spiritually returned") or adjectival (so "your physical and spiritual brother")? Either is permissible from the Greek. Traditional commentary and translation have argued that the phrase is adverbial. Paul has sent the slave Onesimus back to his owner, Philemon, who now has Onesimus back physically (again), but also, because of Onesimus's recent decision to follow Jesus, has found in Onesimus a brother "in the lord." Philemon, then, has received a double bonus from the separation; his slave is now returned, but also returns as a fellow Jesus follower. Presumably, as a Jesus follower, Onesimus would also be a better slave, devoted to his master, honest, willing to serve Philemon as a result of love (*agapē*) and not merely by compulsion. Whatever losses Philemon incurred from the temporary separation are now compensated, not to mention Philemon's expected joy in seeing yet another follower of Jesus. This reading, though traditional, is also the most strained grammatically.

If we take "both in flesh and in lord" as adjectival, it would modify, most reasonably, its closest noun, which in this case is "beloved brother." Paul certainly does use at least one phrase to modify "beloved brother," noting that Onesimus is a beloved brother "especially to me, but much more to you." Clearly, Paul is speaking metaphorically here about *his* relationship to Onesimus. Indeed, as we have noted already, family metaphors in Paul should be assumed to be metaphoric unless there is clear indication otherwise. However, Paul writes that fraternal relation with Onesimus is "even more" the case for Philemon. If being fellow followers of Jesus is indicated by the metaphoric use of "brother," why and how would that be "even more" the case for Philemon? Why and how would Onesimus be "even more" a fellow follower of Jesus for Philemon than for Paul, Onesimus's mentor and guide in the faith? Is Paul alluding to the fact that he guided both men to become Jesus followers? That seems strained.

Onesimus would be "even more" a "brother" for Philemon if Onesimus were *both* Philemon's fellow believer (the metaphorical use of *adelphos*) *and* his actual sibling (Philemon's "brother ... in flesh" or "fleshly brother"). Paul is saying, "You've gotten back your sibling, who is also now your 'brother in Christ.'" Given Paul's normally metaphoric use of *adelphos*, the presence of the words "*en sarchi*" (literally, "in flesh" or "according to flesh") is exactly the sort of rhetorical flag we would need to realize that Paul is not merely using these words metaphorically. Taking "in flesh and in lord" as adjectival has Paul saying in effect: "your brother—both physically and spiritually."

But, as we've said, the language here is "almost … exactly." The phrase "in flesh and in lord," if modifying "brother," is clumsily placed. It could, for example, be modifying "beloved." Also, Paul chooses the Greek word "*agapē*," not "*philos*," for "beloved." Both *agapē* and *philos* could be translated as "love" or "loved one." The Greek "*agapē*" is used to speak of a general sense of regard and care that is centered on another person, similar to the idea of "charity" in English. It does not imply any actual, affective bond. "*Philos*," however, is a word used to describe fraternal love or deep friendship. Paul might also be meaning, through the entire convoluted expression of v. 16, that he shares Philemon's joy of having Onesimus as a fellow believer and a co-worshipper, but not, after sending Onesimus back, Philemon's greater joy (the "even more") of having Onesimus the fellow follower of Jesus (the "brother in the lord") physically present ("in the flesh"). Paul would love Onesimus "in (the) lord," but he could no longer be there physically to express this love to Onesimus; only Philemon could do that.

Paul writes, "No longer a slave, but more than a slave." If, indeed, Philemon and Onesimus were brothers, could Onesimus also be a slave? Could Philemon have owned his sibling? Is *doulos* metaphoric? It certainly could be, yet when considering (1) Onesimus's name, (2) his lack of independent authority (he is sent and received at the command of others), and (3) the focus on his "usefulness," one must admit that understanding Onesimus as a literal slave seems sensible. Moreover, it would not be impossible or unheard of for one sibling to be free and another enslaved. Slavery in the Roman world was governed more by economics than by "race" or genetics. Philemon could also be a former slave who had attained liberty and managed the household's other slaves (including his blood sibling). In such a situation, the freedman might well be supervising—and be responsible for—his still enslaved sibling.

Grammatically, the simplest reading is to take "in flesh" as a modifier for "brother." Yet, in the context of the letter as a whole, this reading would result in a possible but very, very convoluted reconstruction of the letter's context. Which complication is to be preferred: tortured grammar and exegesis of an otherwise clear context or convoluted and complex reconstruction of context through a smoother reading of syntax? Neither alternative is completely satisfying. Were "in flesh" not present, exegesis would be clearer. Were the expression elsewhere in the sentence, exegesis would be clear. Were "slave" not present, exegesis would be clear. Were the comparative modifier "even more" not present but the sentence otherwise standing as it is, exegesis would be clear. Were *philos* present, exegesis would be clear. Were the general context of the letter more specified in writing, exegesis (of this phrase in v. 16, at least) would be clearer. None of this, of course, is the case, and so the ambivalence for us as readers remains. All the alternatives we have mentioned regarding the relationship between Philemon and Onesimus and regarding v. 16 can conceivably and simultaneously be "correct" readings.

Conclusion

Although the letter to Philemon is short and its outline seems simple and straightforward, it is filled with intriguing characters and unresolved questions. Now that we have a basic overview of the letter, let us turn our attention to how the letter has been read or interpreted. We will start with the more established—that is, more traditional—reading in our next chapter.

2

"I Appeal to You for My Child, Onesimus"

As we have seen, Paul's letter to Philemon is the briefest document in the entire collection of writings by Paul. It is one of four letters in the New Testament canon written to an individual and the only personal letter whose Pauline authorship is generally undisputed. The text of Philemon is mostly stable, with just less than a dozen real textual variations and only two or three that are even vaguely significant. (As I have mentioned, the most puzzling variant is whether Paul refers to himself as "an old man" or as an "ambassador" in v. 9; it is understandable if a reader fails to see any real significance in even this difference.) The Greek grammar and vocabulary of Philemon are a bit trickier; there are some modifiers that defy clear association and there are some rare words, but they are not unmanageable. Such brevity, textual stability, lexical particularity, and general clarity would seem to make Philemon straightforward for an interpreter.

It isn't.

As we have also seen, the letter holds several puzzles. Who are Philemon, Apphia, Archippus, and Onesimus? Why is Paul writing to "appeal" to someone? To whom is he writing? Philemon? Apphia? Archippus? All are candidates. The "church" that meets in—presumably—Philemon's, Apphia's, or Archippus's house is the only "character" we can rule out, as the letter addresses a second-person singular "you" for the majority of the time. What is the relationship among the other characters? What damage is Paul concerned about? Precisely what is Paul asking, with some delicacy, to be done (I say "with some" delicacy, but not "with much"). It seems rather rhetorically obvious and yet clumsy to me to write, "I could command you, but I merely ask" (vv. 8–9); the rhetoric implies a request but wraps it like a fish in old papers of coercion and emotional manipulation. Similarly, reminding someone that "you owe me your very life" after having promised to repay any debts (vv. 18–19) strikes me as ungainly manipulation. Some interpreters praise Philemon for being a rhetorical masterpiece. Others, myself among them, cede that it is better rhetoric than many early Christian writings but still find it clumsily obvious in places, painfully obscure in others.

The central problem for interpreting Philemon is not a question of anonymity. The problem is not a mysterious or fragmented textual history. It is not substantially unclear grammar. It is not extended, bulky text or prose. It is the absence of clear and explicit context. Indeed, the clarity of vocabulary, the specificity of addressees, the shortness of the letter all combine to make the context behind Philemon almost inaccessible. The interpretation of Philemon, perhaps more than any other writing associated with the apostle Paul, is dependent upon the reconstruction of context.

Traditional interpretations of Philemon

The letter to Philemon itself does not reveal its immediate circumstances or context, yet both can be clearly found in early Christian commentaries and traditions surrounding the letter. The ancient and dominant view presents Onesimus as an escaped slave, once owned by Philemon. As a renegade, Onesimus encountered Paul (a prisoner) and was led to faith in Jesus of Nazareth as the promised Jewish messiah. Philemon was also a believer, having also been brought to faith by Paul at some earlier time. Paul is now sending Onesimus back to Philemon, but also including a letter that clarifies Onesimus's new faith and (delicately) asks Philemon to be lenient with his now Christ-following slave.

This setting for Philemon is still the predominant reading (e.g. Knox 1937; 1955: 9, 553–55; Koch 1963; Lohse 1971: 186, 189–90; Barth and Blanke 2000: 130; Coursar 2009: 96; cf. Fitzmyer 2000: 12–24; Nordling 2004: 3–19). Very few variations arise among scholars (cf. Knox 1955; Callahan 1997). Some have differed over the precise identity of Apphia and Archippus, with some suggesting that Apphia is Philemon's wife and Archippus his son (and that they are all hosts to an ancient house church). Some argue that Archippus (mentioned also in the letter to the Colossians) actually heads the local congregation to which Philemon belongs. As we have also seen, this tradition about Philemon does resonate with some data within the letter.

The name "Onesimus," roughly translatable as "helpful" or "handy," was a common name for slaves in antiquity. Discussing Onesimus's return as a Jesus follower, Paul assures Philemon that Philemon can now receive back Onesimus "no longer as a slave, but more than a slave, as a brother" (v. 16).

The majority of commentaries agree that Paul wrote the letter to Philemon to intercede for Onesimus (Lohse 1971; Martin 1991; Barth and Blanke 2000; Nordling 2004; Coursar 2009). Indeed, many regard the question as prima facie obvious and seem mildly incredulous that it has ever been challenged, verbally rolling their eyes at the handful of "speculative" and "novel" readings that have been recently advanced. Paul's intercession, called an appeal by *amicus domini* (i.e. a friend of one's benefactor or lord), requires, most argue, that Paul approach the matter obliquely and with some delicacy (this explains Paul's hesitance to command, his reliance upon Philemon's love, his seeming appeal to a past relationship with Philemon, etc.). There is debate about whether Onesimus was captured as a fugitive slave and met Paul in prison, or whether Onesimus sought out Paul for sanctuary, became a Jesus follower and then was sent back to Philemon (cf. Nordling 1991; 2004). Scholarship also differs as to whether Paul is asking Philemon to set Onesimus free or simply not to punish him; this is the area of greatest difference among scholars who adopt the "traditional" reading of Philemon.

Scott Elliott (2011) has argued that Onesimus was not an escaped slave, but had been sent by Philemon as a "gift" to Paul to serve Paul's needs while he was in prison (cf. Winter 1987). With the letter to Philemon, Paul was returning the "gift" and sending Onesimus (whom he had guided to faith in Jesus) back. Paul must do so, however, with real tact. He did not want to imply that Onesimus was unfaithful or causing harm. According to Elliott, Paul was actually refusing a gift from Philemon, since receiving a gift could alter the social standing or the balance of social rank between Philemon and Paul by effectively making Philemon Paul's patron.

These debates aside, there is general consensus among scholars regarding the larger narrative context for Philemon (again, with the notable exception of Knox and Callahan whom we will review in Chapter 3). Barth and Blanke (2000: 1–2) write a summary of this tradition that nearly mirrors the length and complexity of the letter itself.

At first sight the presupposition and intention of the epistle can be summed up as follows: A pagan slaved called Onesimus has run away from his master, Philemon. The owner was a respected member and benefactor of the Christian congregation in the small Asia Minor town of Colossae. The fugitive has found refuge with the apostle Paul, who, in pursuing his missionary work has been imprisoned, probably in a large city. The conditions of Paul's captivity were so liberal as to permit him to benefit from the services that Onesimus, after becoming a Christian, rendered to the propagation of the message of Christ. But while the apostle counts on his own forthcoming release from chains, he sends the slave Onesimus back to his master, together with the letter for Philemon. In grateful recognition of the God-given love and faith that make Philemon a pillar and paragon of the congregation, Paul extends a warm personal plea for the reception of the returning fugitive as a brother. To underline his request the apostle formally pledges to pay in cash for whatever damages are incurred through Onesimus'[s] escape. In addition, Paul expresses the hope that Onesimus might be voluntarily returned to the apostle in order to serve, substituting for Philemon himself, as a permanent helper in the gospel work. Paul hopes to be released in the near future and to visit Philemon. Then he will see with his own eyes whether and how his request has been fulfilled.

They are most confident in the prima facie obviousness of this reading. A bit later they also write:

> There seems to be nothing really new that could be added to observations and evaluations made again and again. Here we will offer no more than a survey of special literary features, especially the attestation, canonization, and integrity, the vocabulary and style, the structure and logic of the text, and the historical-biographical problems related to the main persons mentioned. (103)

Nevertheless, they manage to compose over five hundred pages of commentary. To do so, they spend a great portion of their introduction on issues of slavery in the Roman world. Given the history of interpretation, it has become very difficult indeed to think about Philemon without also thinking about slavery.

Slavery in the Greco-Roman world

Barth and Blanke argue that Paul was acting in congruence with his broader culture. Their review of slavery clarifies that few functioned as free, skilled laborers within the Roman economic systems. Slave labor included unskilled labor but also semi-skilled, skilled, and even professional work. Slave labor could include household management as well as maintenance. Highly skilled managers, artisans, teachers, craftspeople, technicians, and engineers could actually be slaves, so slave work was not limited to unskilled labor of drudgery. Several seminal and contemporary studies have discussed slavery in the Roman world (Zahn 1879; Bömer 1958–63; Urbach 1964; Vogt 1974; cf. Callahan, Horsley and Smith 1998; Byron 2004; Glancy 2006; Avalos 2011).

Roman law had elaborate systems for slave manumission. In some cases slaves were allowed to be independent contractors, selling their labor for additional capital with the ultimate aim of self-redemption. There are records of loyal slaves being manumitted for long-standing service, often at the death of their owner.

Slaves became slaves in a variety of ways. Some were taken as prisoners of war and brought, as captives, into the slave market. Some were, of course, born into slavery. In this case, the slave might be the child of two slaves, the offspring of a slave and the slave's owner or part of an intentional breeding program. Foundlings, orphans, or abandoned children were also frequently taken, raised, and later sold by slave traders. Some slaves entered the slave market because of violent seizure and kidnapping (Morrow 1939: 95–110).

Some individuals seemed to have voluntarily entered slavery, though this was rare and related to two particular phenomena in the Roman world: (1) extreme poverty or poor living conditions; and (2) public sports. Popular arena sports and combat sports contestants in Rome were comprised of slave athletes. These athletes could become so popular that despite risks or shames of slavery, some individuals from various social strata volunteered (Ville 1981: 255; Barton 1993: 26–27). Roman law periodically prohibited the enlistment of citizens from wealthier classes into gladiatorial or athletic slavery.

In some cases, slaves seemed to have been given significant social and personal liberty; some were allowed to select their own cultic practice, to marry and have intact families, to own and manage private property, and to even enjoy public renown. Some appeared to have had the option of living independently or achieving freedom for themselves or for their children (Sokolowski 1954: 122–28; Duff 1958). Recently manumitted slaves, called "freedmen," would certainly enjoy some benefits of independence, even if they were forced, in part, to remain within the employ of former owners (thus becoming de facto indentured servants). During the early Roman imperial period of the first century and a half of the Common Era, there were some voices calling for slave reform (Morrow 1939: 95–110; Barth and Blanke 2000: 33–41, 90–95). Unduly harsh or violent treatment of slaves was discouraged or, in some cases, led to civil penalty (though these were rare and never equaled the penalty for assaulting a free person). A few public intellectuals argued for the dissolution (or de facto dissolution due to restriction) of slavery. There is no question, however, that some slaves during Paul's time were able to enjoy certain measure of public prestige.

Classicists who study ancient slavery, like Barth and Blanke, do acknowledge that there were demerits to being a slave. Social and economic possibilities (not to mention class and social status) could be permanently affected by having been a slave. Slaves possessed no independent legal rights. They could not, on their own, sue or demand legal redress. Abusers who beat or harmed a slave not owned by them could face legal penalty, but only through lawsuit mounted on behalf of the slave's owner for lost labor equity. Slaves were not usually recognized as reliable testimony in court unless tortured. It was largely assumed that no slave had sufficient character to speak truthfully without duress (and, further, that they lacked sufficient character to resist or endure torture). Slaves could be beaten or killed at an owner's whim. Suggestions that this violence would have worked against the economic interests of slave owners (e.g. one does not beat a draft animal to death if one is sensible) don't seem to acknowledge the stigma and psychological toll of knowing that it *could* happen to any slave at any time without recourse (Horsley 1998). Again, there were occasional legal reforms to restrict the violent treatment of slaves, but these are limited and rare; they also suggest that slaves faced real violence (laws normally restrict actions that either actually occurred or most people believe could happen; cf. Bömer 1958–63). Slaves' families could be scattered without any recourse. They could be bred without appeal. They were clearly subjected to psychological, verbal, physical, and sexual abuse regularly. Sex workers in the early Roman era were nearly always slaves (Glancy 2006). Slavery was a form of social death (Patterson 1982).

Comparisons to modern slavery

Barth and Blanke (2000: 4–9) conclude, as do many classicists, that they feel ambivalent about slavery in the Greco-Roman world because of these factors. It was an economic necessity in a preindustrial society, but it could be a way to provide humane shelter and provision for workers. Barth and Blanke openly assert that ancient Greco-Roman slavery was not equivalent to the "chattel slavery" of the American south (or other modern, colonial systems). They suggest that it was, in its more humane provision for unskilled workers and other ways, superior to the extreme exploitations of slaves in early industrial economies. Unlike modern colonial slave systems, slaves in the

Greco-Roman world were not taken because of genotype or "racial" indicators. Economic and political status mattered in one's enslavement; "race" or ethnicity did not (Harrill 1999; 2000). Many classicists note that the pernicious (and clearly tenacious) implications of race-based slavery were not present in ancient Rome. Civil and legal distinctions did apply, for example. Roman citizens could not, without voluntarily renouncing their own freedom and citizenship status, be enslaved. In contrast to colonial, race-based slave systems that arbitrarily created a "slave caste" with unchangeable character traits and often physically visible attributes, Roman slaves were based on legal and economic status. "Race" is, of course, always and only a social construction; it is not "real" in a way that economic or political status is. Still, political and economic status can be concealed to a degree. One can tell at a glance "racial" difference, with this difference creating a permanent subaltern status and contributing to dehumanizing arguments or treatments (cf. Avalos 2011). Roman slavery supposedly avoided these collateral inequalities and evils.

These comparisons are, in my view, neither helpful nor realistic. They work to fundamentally deny the pernicious evil inherent in any form of slavery (cf. Callahan, Horsley and Smith 1998; Johnson, Noel and Williams 2012). There is no moral way to own another human being and force her/him to labor against her/his will. Arguing that Greco-Roman slavery "wasn't so bad" is willfully overlooking faulty comparisons, unequal data, and the reality of abuse (both physical and psychological). It is special pleading. There is a tendency among many to admire the achievements of the Romans. One should ask if Paul's letters accept the reality of slavery (discussed below). Real and terrible experience of modern slavery should inform our impression and reading of both Greco-Roman civilization and Pauline ethics. To argue otherwise is to resist an informed, sober, unwincing view of an ancient evil and, possibly, a silent—indeed, complicit—apostle (Avalos 2011).

Modern slavery is, of course, more documentable and documented. The horrors of modern slavery occurred within an epoch of more widespread literacy and less than two centuries ago. Much of the material and literary evidence, including protest literature, has been preserved. Indeed, archaeology can provide many insights into the living and working conditions of American slaves with a clarity and breadth that classicists can only dream of. We have records of oral lore and public memory from former slaves to flesh out other concrete data; we also have formal, written, and published reports of slavery and how slaves lived during this more recent period of history. In contrast, comparisons of slave conditions often draw from less-than-rigorous constructions of "antiquity," comprised of data from a variety of places, languages, and economic statuses; the experience of the vast, vast majority of slaves is overlooked or perhaps no longer available. When referring to "antiquity," many mean the world we know almost entirely through (extant) literature that surely reflects the views and concerns of the wealthier and more educated slave owners, even though this "antiquity" also spans centuries, diverse regions, and often even different languages. To cite a few examples of well-treated slaves in Greco-Roman literature is not a reasonable or dependable way to construct a complex picture of "slavery in antiquity," nor is it sensible to simply concede the perspective of the slave masters in literature that all slaves are lazy and conniving. Elite Romans might well say that slaves had an enviable time for being "treated well" and without needing to worry about their own provision. Would their slaves under discussion say the same, however? More to the point, whether they did or didn't, the outcome would be the same; as slaves, by definition, they had no say.

Roman households might have grown to love some of their domestic slaves, and those slaves might have appeared grateful, but would the two parties experience the relationship the same way? Elite Roman owners might feel their slaves were not working hard, but would the tired slaves say the same? Elite and educated Roman authors might quip that physical labor was, ultimately, less taxing than the stresses associated with class and status, but I wonder how many slaves would agree. Elite Roman citizens might argue that anyone who was diligent and responsible could, with hard work, achieve freedom and status, but could this be true for any slave? What about the millions of slaves who engaged in hard, responsible labor but remained enslaved, without status, and were basically invisible to an elite Roman?

Certainly, some slaves attained skills and were given important responsibilities by their masters. Without doubt, some slaves occasionally appeared dignified and seemed autonomous in markets and other public spaces. Some domestic slaves, no doubt, grew personal affection for their master or the master's family. Some slaves, almost certainly, preferred their role as slave to working hand-to-mouth as a freedman or indentured servant. However, none of that really matters in slavery. Slaves are slaves. Further, the monumental scale of slavery in the Roman world must be considered. Agricultural, manufacturing, and construction industries were all slave driven. Slaves were, without question, worked to death in quarries and mines; they also had no choice but did what they were told by their masters, whether it was harvesting guano, rowing in galleys, smelting metals, building houses, hauling freight, laboring in shipyards, and more. These slaves became the invisible, teeming, organic machinery of civilization. They awoke well before dawn to spend the hours needed to carry wood, draw water, start and stoke cooking fires, boil eggs, bake bread, clean and set tables and then clear and wash, lay out clothing (which they also mended and washed), and more, all before wealthy patrons strolled out the morning door to business or the baths. In the evenings, slaves hauled refuse, cleaned sewage, fed animals, restocked larders, tended fires, washed and stowed the day's goods, working long after masters had retired for the day. Slaves awoke first, began work before the social day began, hovered in the background of the day's events, and tidied up the day's provisions before stumbling, last, back to bed. Their work was hidden; they remained hidden. Much of their work happened in spaces masters never entered, during hours masters were not home or were asleep; they worked while the masters ate their meals, attended to business, and pursed hobbies. Slaves were to serve and often did so as if they did not exist. Roman mosaics from Pompeii depict men and women having sex while slaves, like a family pet or furniture, stand quietly and invisibly in the corner.

The overwhelming majority of slaves in "antiquity" were unnamed and unknown. Indeed, they as a group tend to be largely *unseen* by the educated, wealthy elites of both the past and the present. As it was true then and is true now, the culture of the wealthy elites is more likely to be preserved. Of those slaves who are named and mentioned in our extant literature, an unfortunately large percentage appear in order to be beaten, whipped, kicked, tortured, or ridiculed. Of those who appear and become visible, a very small portion are spoken of favorably or described (by the elite writers) as enjoying favorable quality of life. The vast majority remain hidden, unknown, organic machines, little more than highly skilled or "usable" livestock.

And from this can we conclude that slavery in "antiquity" was not as egregious as American chattel slavery? One wonders what ancient slaves would make of this claim. When we compare ancient and modern slavery, we are admittedly comparing vastly unequal bodies of evidence. And even here, it is clear that the experience of slavery in antebellum America, for example, was not uniform (Lewis 1991; Horsley 1998; Harrill 2000). Some slaves were educated; they conducted and managed business ventures and were given some autonomy. Some slaves were given domestic duties; though their labor was manual, they were provided with adequate clothing and comfortable environs. Some slaves were chattel, working in malaria-infested fields under grueling conditions for unreasonable hours and forced to live in substandard housing with inadequate provisions and clothing. Indeed, a single estate could have slaves in all these roles. Some slave masters were gentle, some were harsh and violent; the majority were likely indifferent. It would not be difficult to imagine just as much complexity and diversity among slaves in "antiquity." To argue whether ancient or modern slave systems are "worse" is to engage in an absurd game of misery poker, while using only scraps of evidence to construct arguments that, ultimately, seem like special pleading. As the notable social scientist Orlando Patterson (1982: 13) has observed, slavery is a form of social death. Slaves are erased from social reality. "Slavery," as some scholars put it, "is a species of social murder. It reduces human life to a travesty of itself, sacrifices human beings on the altar of violent desire" (Callahan, Horsley and Smith 1998: 1). Debating about whether one might choose one era of slavery over another, or whether one might choose to be an elite slave instead of a struggling freedman misses a key point: slaves have no choice. Every life choice is made for them. They have no rights. They have no recourses. They are given no redress.

While more slaves during the New Testament times seemed to have "semi-professional" status and more opportunity for eventual release (manumission of slaves was not uncommon under Roman law), one should remember that a substantially higher percentage of the population, probably the majority, were slaves during this time than, say, antebellum America. Further, differences between slave and non-slave in the Greco-Roman world were still understood as the result of innate "nature" or character. Unlike racially driven slave systems which argue that a particular race of people is inferior and unable to self-govern, Roman-style slave systems that were based on status and economics argued that the wealthy were innately better; that is, they possessed greater independence, intelligence, will, and general "gumption." Slaves in the Roman world would have been deemed inferior in essence for having allowed or tolerated enslavement, unable to control their bodies or financial resources. Perversely, the fact *that* they were slaves proved the rightness of their enslavement (Joshel 1986; 1992; Hopkins 1993).

The algorithm linking slavery to character flaw, on the one hand, and freedom to superior character, on the other, appears as a common trope in the literature of antiquity. Given its ubiquity, slavery often was employed as rhetorical illustration and intellectual metaphor. Slaves, again and again, are pictured as comic buffoons, lazy, devious, treacherous, slovenly, lecherous, and dull witted. Masters and their domestic slaves might develop a fondness for each other, but this affection was often set within a context of paternalism. The slaves were unable to love as equals. In Roman hierarchies of social power and virtue, slaves always lost.

Paul and slavery

Philosophical literature occasionally problematizes this negative representation of slavery (Barth and Blanke 2000; cf. Seneca, *Ep.* 47; *Ben.* 2.18; 3.22). The most frequent trope here is the metaphoric comparison of slavery to the philosopher's driving passion for knowledge or truth. Independence and self-control are lost in the longing for the (sometimes cruel) master of learning and insight. In contrast, the nonphilosophical are often described as being enslaved to physical passions. Stoics seem particularly interested in slaves, arguing for the virtue of the "good slave," likening themselves as "slaves" to reason and, even more often, non-Stoics to slaves of passion. Stoics also, from an early point, advocated for fair treatment of slaves (Plato, *Prt.* 337C; *Plt.* 1.338a–340c; Xenophon, *Hell.* 2.3.48).

Paul, perhaps influenced by the Greek philosophers, uses slavery as a metaphor as well (Martin 1990; Barclay 1991; Engberg-Pedersen 2000; Glancy 2006: 39–70). Paul frequently refers to himself or to others as *diakonoi* (sing. *diakonos*) or *douloi* (sing. *doulos*). He does this in Philemon. The former term is frequently translated "servant," the latter more directly as "slave." In many places, *diakonos* is also translated "minister" or transliterated "deacon." *Diakonos* has a nuanced meaning of "table" and hence that of a "household servant." Its use as a description for service to another person within early Christian communities was pervasive enough that the term becomes the title for a standing church office. This transition is visible across the writings attributed to Paul. *Doulos* is a more generic term for "slave." It can (but does not always) designate unskilled, often very physical, manual labor. It does, however, suggest a sense of difficult work and lowly status. Paul uses the term to refer to himself in his writings, particularly when he is pursuing a point about his own insignificant state before God (Rom. 1.1; 2 Cor. 4.5; Gal. 1.10; Phil. 1.1).

There are other terms for "slave" in ancient Greek. Many noting a particular nuance of slave function or work, others simply designate the subordinate, nonhuman state of slaves, often very dramatically (Bradley 1994). *Pais* or *paidos*, for example, is often translated as "boy" or "child," but it can also be a somewhat sharp designation for one's slave (e.g. Luke 7.7). *Soma*, or literally "body," is yet another term that graphically designates the nonpersonhood of slaves (e.g. Rev. 18.13). To be in service as slaves is metaphorically to be "under the yoke," like a beast of burden (e.g. 1 Tim. 6.1); in fact, animal metaphors for slavery are not uncommon (Bradley 1990; 2000). As Antoinette Wire (1990: 73–79) has noted, seeing a slave as a mere "body" or "vessel" also had overtones of sexual exploitation, particularly that of slaves; these are not absent from Pauline vocabulary generally or from Philemon (Marchal 2011). Paul's language at 1 Thess. 4.4—where sexual desire is to be quelled by finding an appropriate "vessel" for it—may suggest that sex with slaves is viewed as immaterial or inconsequential by Paul. "Useful" (the same word Paul uses in Phlm 11) is also slang and euphemism for sex with a slave in Greek outside the New Testament. It is significant to note how these various terms feature either the slave's body or the slave's productivity. The slave's personhood—her/his ideas, feelings, desires—are irrelevant. It implies—indeed, emphasizes—a status of complete subservience.

When Paul designates himself as a "slave" (Rom. 1.1; 2 Cor. 4.5; Gal. 1.10; Phil. 1.1), he is making an explicit and dramatic comment about his status before God. His parallel and model is Jesus who, he argues, surrendered sovereignty over his own body to be tortured to death (Philippians 2). Is Paul articulating that he does not control his own travel, occupation, or life situation? Is Paul aware of the darker dimensions of the slave system?

Paul's most frequent term for Jesus, apart from *christos* ("anointed one" or "christ") is "lord" (*kurios*). This is certainly true in Philemon. *Kurios* is not primarily a theological or political designation. Its most common sense is "master." It is, I would argue, at base a term of power, reflecting seriously status differentials rooted in economics. Paul likens the life of the believer to being enslaved by God. A common term by Paul for justification (i.e. being brought back into relationship with God) is "redemption." This word, also an economic term, is equally well translated as "purchased" or "manumitted." God through Jesus, in Paul's thinking, has purchased believers back from enslavement to sin (e.g. 1 Cor. 6.20). Slavery is the normal status for humans; pure freedom is not possible (Rom. 6.1–14).

In addition to using slavery as a metaphor for spiritual transition or transformation, Paul also addresses the reality of slaves in households. In 1 Corinthians, Paul advises any believers who are also slaves to be content with the lot they have been given by God and to serve God and their master(s) faithfully (1 Cor. 7.21–24). Should freedom become available, one ought to seize upon it; it will enable one to be more versatile in service toward God. One ought not, however, to actively pursue freedom. This pursuit will drain one's resources and produce distraction. Slave metaphors and support for slave systems can also be found in the deutero- or pseudo-Pauline traditions. Slaves are also addressed in a debated letter like Colossians. Slaves are told in that letter to serve their masters "in everything" with "reverence for the lord" or for the "master" (Col. 3.22–28). Masters should treat slaves "right and fair"; this, however, should be clarified. Treating slaves justly may mean simply that masters "ought" to treat them in ways that are considered appropriate to treat slaves. Masters are also reminded that they are, in turn, God's slaves (Col. 4.1).

Paul, the loyalist Jew from the diaspora who is also known as the "apostle to the Gentiles," very famously reflects a hybridization between Greco-Roman ways of thinking and Jewish practice (cf. Mendelsohn 1949). Certain passages from the Hebrew Bible limit the violence done to slaves. For example, runaway slaves must be given shelter and not returned (Deut. 23.15–16). Slaves injured by beatings or death can receive recompense (though not at the rate of a free person being violently treated in the same manner; cf. Exod. 21.20–21, 26–27). Female slaves who were raped must be given the option of marriage or provided for as an unwanted spouse (Deut. 21.10–14). Slaves who are Israelite can anticipate freedom after a period of indentured servitude (Exod. 21.1–5; Lev. 25.44–46, 48–54; Deut. 15.12–18). Family connections also limit, to a degree, potential enslavement, or sexual exploitation (Exod. 21.7–8; Lev. 25.39). Slaves are to be circumcised and are required to abstain from idolatry (Gen. 17.13; 27); they enjoy less religious liberty and can be conscripted into "conversion." At the same time, capture and resale of Israelite slaves are limited (Exod. 21.7–11; Deut. 24.7). Their Israelite status further entitles them to certain rights; most notably, at least according to biblical text, they cannot be forced to work on Sabbaths and feast days (e.g. Exod. 20.10). There is, however, little explicit indication that Jews in the early Roman Empire circumcised their household slaves; given Roman views on circumcision as mutilation, it is difficult to imagine such a practice could escape general comment if it were widely practiced among Jews.

In both Palestine and the diaspora, it is clear that Jews in the Second Temple period had slaves. It remains unclear how much or how widely the restrictions from Hebrew biblical texts were applied and followed. Doubtless, oral law and local tradition addressed variations and established particular norms in practice. Yet, equally clear, Jews who intended to articulate their Jewishness in daily practice must have dealt with these biblical texts in some practical way. Biblical text would have—should have—informed Paul's thinking in some way.

Paul clearly has inherited generic Jewish language and metaphorically likened God's deliverance to redemption from slavery (cf. Romans 5). Paul's notions about the escape from being "slaves to sin" in Romans would seem to reflect the Exodus narrative of God's establishment of a covenant people via liberation from bondage and slavery. For Jews, Sabbath observance was (and is) a marker of liberation and redemption. It was linked to notions of inheritance and rest. Paul roots sanctification via identification with Jesus as Christ in similar ways. How then might Hebrew Scriptures influence Paul's view on slavery?

Philemon, Paul, and the ethics of slavery

Scholars who understand Onesimus as a slave debate whether Paul is arguing for the gentle reception or the full manumission of Onesimus. Critical is Paul's intent in asking Philemon to receive Onesimus "no longer as a slave, but as a brother." Someone with knowledge of what the Hebrew Scriptures say about slavery would not necessarily see sharing a religion with one's slaves as incompatible. As we have seen, slavery of fellow Jews is discouraged in Hebrew Scriptures (and regulated to the extent that it becomes de facto indentured servitude), but the circumcision of household male slaves and the inclusion of slaves in mandated festivals could legitimize not only possession of slaves but also rudimentary or even compulsory "conversion" of slaves.

Paul's pragmatism and indifference

The suggestion that Paul believes it moral for Philemon to manumit Onesimus but feels the step "too delicate" to articulate clearly implies an almost laughable unfamiliarity with Paul. When matched with other statements by Paul on slavery, moments when he is addressing domestic or economic practices and not merely being metaphorical, Paul does not regard slave ownership as prima facie immoral. He seems remarkably indifferent to slavery as in his other letters. If Onesimus's status as a slave is assumed, then Paul might very well be using oblique rhetoric because he grants Philemon the right to be harsh with Onesimus or to keep Onesimus enslaved. Paul may hope for a different outcome, but seems to accede to the potential that things may not turn out the way he prefers. Paul would then, in fact, be saying, "I wish you wouldn't, but you've got the right, I guess."

If Paul is trying to talk Philemon out of excessive anger or violent reprisal, one may wish (particularly if one were Onesimus) for Paul to do so both directly and assertively. Paul may not be anticipating a potential beating for

Onesimus, but, instead, be asking for Onesimus's return to Paul's service. One wonders here, however, if Paul is really thinking through the potential implications of slave-master relationships; after all, he is still regarding and featuring Onesimus as "useful."

Whatever conclusion we draw regarding Paul's "entreaty" or request on Onesimus's behalf, it remains clear that Paul is largely indifferent to (let us assume, for now) Onesimus's status as a slave. His focus is on a pragmatic outcome, his facile equation of slavery with virtue (i.e. submission to Jesus), his linkage of work with worth, and his disinterest in any explicit discussion of slave status match readily with the Paul of Romans, Corinthians, and the disputed letter to the Colossians.

Paul seems as manipulative of Philemon as he is oblique in his request of him. Paul asks Philemon to act of his own accord, but he does so after reminding Philemon of Paul's rights to outright command. Paul writes the letter about a personal matter with an introduction that includes a small crowd of witnesses (i.e. "the church that meets in your house"); he is speaking to Philemon about a private matter in a very, very public way. Paul offers to remit debts, but only after reminding Philemon of the greater debt Philemon owes Paul and how Paul has simply forgiven it. Paul expresses his confidence in Philemon's "obedience," thus suggesting, in his word choice, that at some level Paul feels he has made something more than a polite request to a friend. Paul clearly does not consider Philemon his equal but feels comfortable and appropriate to use passive aggressive rhetoric to manipulate Philemon and put him "on the spot."

Most scholars today agree that Paul's real request here is being veiled but is, in fact, rather forceful; they also agree that Paul's oblique and forceful rhetoric are related. Modern, post-1870 scholars have largely argued that Paul is attempting to end slavery: Paul is calling for the manumission of Onesimus (and, by example, all slaves), though his is a "slant" request, asking for one case and doing so in a very veiled way. Prior to the American Civil War, however, the majority of scholars saw, with equal clarity, that Paul was disinterested in slavery and found it morally neutral. Both sides argued its position pointing to the same text and to Paul's oblique rhetoric.

A middle position could also be articulated. Paul may be indifferent toward slavery as an institution. His main request is that Onesimus be returned to Paul as a coworker and helper. If that can be accomplished via manumission, Paul wants that. If it can be done by another means, Paul is fine with that too. Paul is not direct in his rhetoric or his request because he is (*pace* Elliott 2011) asking for a (financial) gift. Onesimus and his fate are of secondary interest to Paul. Read this way, Onesimus as a person with agency, feelings, and desires vanishes from the letter rather quickly. Even when named, Onesimus is significant largely because of his association with someone else—with Jesus, with Paul or with Philemon. Onesimus, on his own terms, is less interesting and less important to Paul. While being unconcerned with the plight of a slave may seem callous to modern readers of Paul, this is not beyond his general cultural context. To expect him to be anything otherwise seems, in a way, to border on being an unfair expectation. In any case, more than a few *modern* scholars have also lost sight of the actual slaves in antiquity, seeing slavery in Paul's time as either a regrettable economic necessity or a situation which really, in the end, was tolerable (particularly in how it was different from later slave systems). For most readers, Paul and Philemon overshadow Onesimus and become more interesting figures in the letter. Such, sadly, is the inevitable erasure of the slave (and why slavery can never be morally neutral).

Ethics of interpretation

Some have argued that the Bible tolerates the reality of slavery in order to foster attention to more important principles for reform. For example, Rodney Stark (2007) has argued that the Bible is intentionally subversive; its principles would gradually and inevitably lead to slavery's dissolution. Rather than act outright in condemnation, the biblical authors silently let the camel's nose of moral reform into the tent, knowing that slavery will dissolve in time. Stark and others have also argued that any moral reforms of the Western world are traceable directly to the influence of the Bible; we live in the moral world we do today (such that we do) solely as a result of the Bible.

In contrast, Hector Avalos laments in his book *Slavery, Abolition, Biblical Scholarship* (2011) how many biblical and classical scholars have worked to actively misread the Bible's clear, emphatic, and uniform endorsement of slavery. The Bible not only emerged from a world in which slavery was common, but it also integrates slavery into its worldview, its metaphors, and its very structure. For Avalos, the "plain sense" of the biblical text (meaning, for him, the best reconstructed historical and grammatical reading of the author's intention) endorses slavery, even though others, such as Richard Horsley and Allen Callahan, deny the "plain sense" of the Bible and argue that it opposes slavery. Avalos dismisses all the readings he surveys as "misreadings."

Avalos is critical of those who argue that slavery in the ancient Near East or the early Roman Empire was qualitatively different from slavery of later periods. While differences were present, the essential trauma of one human owning another remains consistent. According to Avalos, there is fundamentally no way for a human being to own another human being ethically. Slavery as a system is always already immoral. That the Bible does not articulate this, indeed that it goes further to not only assume but also endorse the necessity of slavery, is a paramount failing of biblical ethics, and one which, Avalos argues, biblical scholars have not been quick to note.

Sex and slavery

Avalos's arguments are astute and challenging. One must question, however, when he continues to argue that biblical scholars, on the whole, are ignoring the problem of slavery in the Bible or are "misreading" it. Several very fine scholars have foregrounded the reality of slavery in the Bible as well as the ethical and interpretive challenges it poses.

One scholar in particular addresses the problem of the Bible's tacit endorsement of slavery head on. Jennifer Glancy's *Slavery in the New Testament* (2006) attempts to provide a full picture of Greco-Roman slave systems and their implications upon ethics. Glancy focuses on ethics related to embodiment issues that surrounded Greco-Roman slavery. The way power inequality was expressed in and upon enslaved bodies parallels a similar concern that feminists have regarding patriarchy. Slaves lost control of their own bodies in their vulnerability to abuse or sexual exploitation as well as in their need to perform routine domestic work at the mercy of their master's bidding. Indeed, the "routine work" of many slaves involved physical and sexual abuse of their bodies by others.

Glancy unpacks at length issues surrounding sexual use and abuse of slaves. Slaves were paired or "bred" for economic purposes. Sex workers in the Greco-Roman world were nearly always enslaved, as were gladiators. The use of a human body for another's pleasure, like the use of another's body for one's labor and productivity, was integral to Greco-Roman slavery. In light of this, Glancy notes not only the absence of critique against slavery in New Testament texts but also the tacit acceptance and even use of slavery as a central metaphor by New Testament writers. The silence of the New Testament about slavery becomes thunderously loud.

Just as Glancy correlates Greco-Roman slavery and the ethical problems it produced to a feminist critique of power and exploitation, Joseph Marchal (2011) also applies feminist, gender, and queer criticism to his reading of slavery in the New Testament. Drawing from the French philosopher Michel Foucault, Marchal notes how social hierarchy in antiquity also resulted in hierarchically constructed gender norms that enabled the use of another's body for one's own sexual pleasure. "Maleness" exerted power over other, more recessive identities. Power over another's body—particularly power used for one's own pleasure—was indicative of status and "masculinity." Marchal argues, then, for a correlation among sexual exploitation, sex work and slave systems in antiquity. To put it bluntly, slaves were always already sexual victims. As mentioned above, Marchal observes that Paul's pun for Onesimus being "useful" has sexual connotations, especially given Onesimus's status as a slave. Paul's "pun" could be construed as, at best, remarkably insensitive to how an enslaved Onesimus would hear it, given how the word was so immediately and pervasively tied to sexual exploitation of slaves. That so many modern commentators take delight in Paul's little pun without even a second thought as to how an enslaved Onesimus might hear it is also telling. It indicates the callousness of Paul, and perhaps that of others, toward the plight of the enslaved. Marchal's arguments, along with Glancy's, should intensify the moral problems Philemon presents to modern readers (cf. Wire 1990).

Conclusion

Paul's call in Philemon for love, for "fellow workers" (vv. 1, 24), for "fellow-ship in arms" (v. 2) could have—should have?—foregrounded the reality of the exploited slaves in Paul's world, as well as led its readers to consider the de facto slavery and the frequent physical and sexual exploitation of the poor and the week in the modern world. Unfortunately, actual slavery (like sexual exploitation of the powerless) still exists. What most traditional readings of Philemon that assume Onesimus's slave status fail to confront is Paul's failure to recognize the humanity of the other: Paul fails Onesimus, who is worthwhile to others only because he is now "useful." We have no idea in this letter of Onesimus's wants or feelings. Many of these traditional readings also suggest that Onseimus was the laborer carrying the letter from Paul that so blithely comments upon his "usefulness" but hesitates to command his freedom. If so, Onesimus, as always, found himself in the role of the bound, the servant in the corner, the hidden laborer; he was silent, unseen, awaiting the execution of his task. If he had any thoughts or ideas, they were the only things that he could—and must—keep for himself.

3

Rethinking Onesimus and Philemon

Philemon, as we have seen, has been interpreted by many as an appeal by Paul to Philemon on behalf of an escaped slave, now a convert to Christianity, named Onesimus. Paul is sending the new convert back to his owner Philemon. As we have also seen, this narrative can be taken as a background context for the letter and produce a sensible reading. But from where does this narrative arise in the first place? Is it the only possible reading of Philemon? Is this reconstructed context necessarily implied by the contents of the letter? If it isn't, why is it so widely accepted?

As we have also seen, there is no indication in the letter at all that Onesimus is an escaped slave or that he has done any actual harm to Philemon (let alone that he stole or damaged property in his escape). Indeed, on close reading and reflection, we cannot be altogether certain that Philemon is even the principal addressee of the letter or that Onesimus is even a slave.

Troubling the "standard reading": John Knox and modern reimaginings

Commentaries and homilies on Philemon, for centuries, have assumed a "standard reading" of the events behind Philemon, but scholarship of the nineteenth and twentieth centuries problematized these readings, exposing the depth of assumptions and unfounded reconstructions inherent within them. F. C. Baur, for example, reviewed the text of Philemon, noting Philemon has a striking number of *hapax legomena* (i.e. words that are used only once in the canon). Philemon's context vis-à-vis its setting in and its relationship to Paul's life is uncertain; the letter also references characters otherwise unknown. It has problematic theological implications and fits issues pertinent to Christians much later than Paul. These Baur also set against a marked hesitance by early Christians to refer to this letter to Philemon (some also seeming to refer to it by another title, the lost letter to the "Laodiceans"). He concluded, using these same criteria that he applied to his study of the authorship of the Pastorals, that Philemon was not originally Pauline at all (Baur 1875).

I will have more to say about Baur's work in the next chapter; however, let me point out now that other scholars in the twentieth century also probed the assumptions inherent in the interpretive or receptive history regarding Philemon. John Knox (1955; 1959), for example, argues aggressively that a very different understanding of events behind Philemon was required.

> [O]nce we decide that the note was written to the master of a runaway slave, we are likely to feel that we possess the only clue needed for its interpretation. But in doing so we are taking quite too much for granted ... It is my conviction that this presupposition has often resulted in serious distortion of the otherwise plain meaning of the note. (Knox 1959: 18)

For Knox, reading of Onesimus's escape, damages to his owner, and even repentance are all questionable assumptions.

Not quite the parallel

Knox cites a familiar and parallel letter of petition written by Pliny the Younger to Sabinianus on behalf of Sabinianus's freedman. We don't know much about Sabinianus, but quite a bit about Pliny the Younger (his father, Pliny the Elder, was a prominent intellectual and naturalist who died investigating Mount Vesuvius). He was a Roman governor of the Roman province of Bithynia (central Turkey) from 111 to 113 CE. Much of his official and personal correspondence has been preserved. These letters not only provide a window into Roman provincial bureaucracy but also include the first extant mention of Christianity by a nonbeliever (*Ep.* 10.96–97). Pliny, as governor, often arbitrated minor disputes, particularly among his social clients. Sabinianus was one of Pliny's clients.

In this case, a conflict had arisen. Sabinianus's freedman had fled, but, when cooler heads prevailed, the freedman wished to return home. Pliny was writing as an intermediary between the two men. Roman society was greatly stratified. In many ways, it was an elaborate patron-client system all the way up a socioeconomic pyramid that terminated in the emperor himself; within this system, individuals lived out various loyalties to their social and economic patrons. In addition to being benevolent to their clients who were below them in the pyramid, patrons often negotiated settlements and arbitrated among various clients. Sabinianus's freedman had obviously approached Pliny, Sabinianus's social superior and patron, for arbitration; Pliny obliged and intervened. A second, later letter indicates that Pliny's intercession was successful.

This letter has long been seen as a parallel to the social situation of Philemon, as least as it has traditionally been assumed. The letter is brief and can be repeated in full here. It reads:

> To Sabinianus. The Freedman of yours with whom you said you were angry has been to me, flung himself at my feet, and clung to me as if I were you. He begged my help with many tears, though he left a good deal unsaid; in short, he convinced me of his genuine penitence. I believe he has reformed, because he realizes he did wrong. You are angry, I know, and I know too that your anger was deserved, but mercy wins most praise when there was just cause for anger. You loved the man once, and I hope you will love him again, but it is sufficient for the moment if you allow yourself to be appeased. You can always be angry again if he deserves it, and will have more excuse if you were once placated. Make some concession to his youth, his tears, and your own kind heart, and do not torment him or yourself any longer—anger can only be torment to your gentle self. I am afraid you will think that I am using pressure, not persuasion, if I add my prayers to his—but this is what I shall do, and all the more freely and fully because I have given the man a severe scolding and warned him firmly that I will never make such a request again. This is because he deserved a fright, and it is not intended for your ears; for maybe I shall make another request and obtain it, as long as it is not unsuitable for me to ask and you to grant. (Pliny the Younger, *Ep.* 9.21 LCL)

The affinities to Philemon are obvious. Yet they are also few, especially when one reads carefully. Indeed, there are very serious differences, as Knox notes. First, Sabinianus's freedman in Pliny's letter is neither a runaway nor a slave; he is a freedman whose actions has damaged the interests of his patron. Second, most obviously, Pliny intercedes by specifically asking Sabinianus for forgiveness. Notably, Paul never explicitly requests the same for Philemon on behalf of Onesimus. It seems odd that Paul, if he is indeed interceding on behalf of an escapee, never once expresses Onesimus's sorrow or asks for Philemon's forgiveness, while both are integral elements in Pliny's intercessory letter. Indeed, the whole point of the intercessory letter (if Pliny's can be taken as its exemplar) is intercession, something Paul's letter to Philemon never quite fully does (cf. Russell 1998).

Not just a slave

Knox suggests that Paul was indeed sending Onesimus back, but not returning an escaped slave. In some ways, Knox's argument is similar to that of Elliott (2011) mentioned in the last chapter. According to Knox, Paul was sending Onesimus, who had been serving him while Paul was incarcerated, along with Paul's other delegates (principally Timothy) to Colossae. Knox differs from Elliott by avoiding Elliott's reconstructions of patron-client privilege. Instead, Knox recalls Paul's practice of sending his letters to various communities via a trusted coworker who could also correctly explicate Paul's remarks and perhaps even offer a persuasive appendix to his remarks in oral argument. Knox suggests that Paul would like his letter, being carried to Colossae by Onesimus and Timothy, to be well received, but anticipated a potential problem. Drawing from the unusual Greek syntax in the first two verses of Philemon as well as their parallels in Colossians, Knox concludes that the principal addressee in Paul's personal letter—and Onesimus's owner—is actually Archippus (since Paul also gives a special instruction to Archippus in Col. 4.17). According to Knox, Paul is asking Archippus to return Onesimus to Paul's service, ideally as a manumitted freedman.

Knox next surveys the history of Philemon's canonization and particularly notes E. R. Goodenough's (1929; 1933) argument that Ephesians is an expansion of Colossians to function as a "cover-letter" introduction to the canonical Pauline corpus. For Knox, attempts to collect and create a Pauline corpus reflect a critical moment in early Christianity. Further, the fact that this short letter to Philemon about a private matter persisted among early collections proves its significance. The persistent inclusion of Philemon in the canon, despite many third-century assessments that it was insignificant, points to an earlier, larger, extra-canonical motivation and significance.

Knox argues that the Onesimus mentioned in Philemon is the same figure addressed as bishop in Ignatius's early second-century epistle to the Ephesians (*Eph.* 1.3; 2.1; 6.2); this Onesimus is also, for Knox, the same Onesimus who is mentioned in Col. 4.7–9, where reference to Onesimus's freedom of travel would strongly preclude his fugitive status (cf. Harrison 1950: 288–93, where he suggests that Onesimus is also the Onesiphorus mentioned in 2 Tim. 1.16–18; see also Fitzmyer 2000: 13–17). Knox suggests that Archippus acceded to Paul's arguments and released Onesimus, and

Onesimus went on to become an important figure in early Christianity as the bishop at Ephesus. Accepting Goodenough's argument that the Pauline corpus was collected in ancient Ephesus, Knox argues that Onesimus must have supervised this collection, including the incorporation of Philemon and the preparation of Ephesians (cf. Gamble 1975).

Not so obvious

Knox's work reveals the breadth and complexity of assumptions about the setting and context of Philemon. And his reading, quite frankly, "works." It accounts for much of the data and produces a reasonable and plausible historical reconstruction that also resonates with some of the received Christian traditions. It exemplifies how one can refute or invert nearly every element of the traditional reconstructed context behind Philemon and still produce an effective, coherent, and plausible interpretation of the letter.

Subsequent scholarship has, however, not found Knox compelling. Generally, his arguments are dismissed as conjecture. Occasionally, he is criticized for arguments he does not make. Eduard Lohse (1971: 186), for example, misrepresents Knox's rationale for identifying Archippus as the letter's primary recipient by omitting Knox's significant grammatical analysis of vv. 2–3. Lohse also neglects Knox's use of patristic literature and testimony in his argument for the role of Philemon in the New Testament canon. Allen Callahan (1997) notes that Knox reveals significant and suspicious assumptions in the traditional and "standard reading" of Philemon, but considers Knox's arguments ultimately marred by his eclectic views about Onesimus and the collection of the Pauline writings. Few who dismiss Knox as "too much conjecture," however, seem as willing as Callahan to acknowledge how much conjecture lies beneath the traditional reading of Onesimus as a runaway slave. Knox reveals how different assumptions can lead to different reconstructions of Philemon's story. This revelation is often met by an appeal to the antiquity and uniformity of "the tradition" surrounding Philemon (Lohmeyer 1964; Lohse 1971; Bruce 1984; Connolly 1987; Nordling 1991; Rapske 1991; Dunn 1996; Barth and Blanke 2000; Coursar 2009; Harris 2010). Such an appeal would be most persuasive if the "standard reading" were really shown to be both broad and ancient. Yet, the source of nearly every assumption beneath that traditional reading—in fact, the source of that traditional reading itself—can be traced back to the work of John Chrysostom in his fourth-century homilies on Philemon (cf. Callahan 1993; 1995; 1997; Mitchell 1995).

John Chrysostom and the patristic reading of Philemon

Prior to Chrysostom, Philemon languished in Pauline scholarship because of its perceived insignificance. Chrysostom's series of homilies on Philemon (Schaff 1994) did not occur in a cultural vacuum. In Chrysostom's Constantinople, Christianity faced a substantial social conundrum. Chrysostom wanted a Christianity that was compatible with social conservatism in order to maintain the movement's political and civic reputation. As Callahan (1997: 15) notes, Chrysostom placed himself within the "master class" of the social division of slavery and might well want to preserve his own social status and interests. Yet Chrysostom was also concerned with the sexual exploitation of slaves; this might even have been his chief concern. Chrysostom wanted a means of restricting slave abuses (because of his sense of Christian ethics) while also permitting the institution of slavery itself to continue (because of his desire to merge Christianity with social conservatism).

In his reading of Philemon, Chrysostom sees Paul as complying with expectations (sending Onesimus back) but also implicitly suggesting that Onesimus must not be harshly treated and perhaps even hinting that Onesimus should be manumitted. Doing so, Chrysostom could begin to construct homilies that reinforced conservative social norms (perpetuating slavery) but simultaneously restricting what he considered abuses (violence or sexual assault against converted slaves).

In other words, Chrysostom is the one who explicitly articulated the "escaped slave" narrative for the first time; it appears to be his own idea, generated essentially whole cloth from his own readings that were, no doubt, heavily influenced by his own, immediate social needs (Pearson 1999). There is no clear evidence of any similar readings prior to Chrysostom (Callahan 1995). Chrysostom cites no source or reference, presenting his work on Philemon as simply the "obvious" reading. Scholarship has largely concurred for over a millennium.

Several assumptions in Chrysostom's readings need exposed. First, it is implausible that an escaped slave who happened to be in flight from one of Paul's converts would coincidentally be incarcerated alongside Paul (*pace* Nordling 1991). The implausibility here is magnified by the fact that Roman civil law would not have incarcerated Onesimus but would have transported him as quickly as possible to his rightful owner. Even granting that the highly implausible could happen (as, indeed, we have learned in many historical narratives), there is no indication in the letter that Onesimus has escaped. Certainly, Paul promises that *if* any costs are associated with Onesimus, Paul will make them good (v. 18). This can, of course, pertain to an escape (and Onesimus may have stolen or damaged property in his flight) or just to Onesimus's absence or his debt that caused his enslavement in the first place. A person could also incur debts and damages without being a slave (I have incurred both and I suspect the same for most readers). To complicate the picture further, the grammatical structure of Paul's sentence in v. 18 suggests that the hypothetical protasis ("if he has incurred any damages") isn't likely or is less likely than the main consequent clause or apodosis (i.e. Paul's promise to repay). The sense of the sentence is something like: "If there happen to be any outstanding debts, you may be sure that I will repay."

Furthermore, as inscriptional evidence reveals, "Onesimus" is not a name used only for slaves (Connolly 1987; Artz-Grabner 2001). From inscriptional (not literary) evidence, one could argue that the name does not belong to a slave in the majority of its occurrences. In addition, even if Onesimus was a slave at some point in his life, he could have been manumitted and become a freedman under Roman law before Paul wrote Philemon. If freed by Philemon, or perhaps Philemon's father, Onesimus would still have obligations to Philemon's household (cf. Connally 1987; Vos 2001). Indentured to Philemon, it is very, very possible that Onesimus could have become derelict in his duties, at least according to Philemon's assessment. Though not without consequence, this would still be very different from the scenario assumed by the "standard reading." Indeed, freedmen often had to endure real limits upon their economic and practical liberties; they were, however, generally at greater liberty and more legally protected than slaves.

Onesimus is referred to as a slave indirectly in v. 16 ("no longer as a slave, but more than a slave"). As we have noted, Paul does use "slave" or "servant" to designate followers of Jesus and himself, and he almost always does so as a metaphor (the only exception seems to be when Paul is discussing his rules for household management, such as 1 Corinthians 2 or, if written by Paul, Col. 3.12–4.1). In Philemon, Paul also refers to Onesimus metaphorically as his "child" (v. 10). No one assumes from this that Paul was the biological or adopted father of Onesimus. Paul makes note of his "fellow workers" (vv. 1, 24). Again, this is a common trope and no one, to my knowledge, reads this to mean that Paul and those he mentioned were once financially employed by the same person. Paul, finally, refers to Archippus as his "fellow soldier"

(v. 2); similarly, no one has ever suggested that Paul and Archippus were veterans from the same military force.

As we have seen, Paul goes on in v. 16 to entreat that Onesimus be received "not as a slave" but "as a beloved brother." Sibling metaphors do indicate ideological or theological affiliation, both in Paul and in general philosophical discourse. Paul may be signifying Onesimus here as Philemon's ideological or theological brother. His return and presence with Philemon "in the flesh" (i.e. being physically with Philemon) will bring Philemon the greater joy because Onesimus is "with" Philemon both ideologically or theologically ("in [the] lord") and physically ("in [the] flesh"). Yet, why does Chrysostom (and a host of later interpreters) regard "slave" as obviously literal but "brother" as equally obviously metaphoric, particularly since the latter ("brother") is immediately next to the modifying "in the flesh" and "in [the] lord" (not only "in [the] lord")?

For reasons we have already discussed in Chapter 1, the simpler reading of this expression is arguably that Onesimus and Philemon are siblings. Philemon's joy will be greater because he has the companionship again of someone who is not only his biological or legal brother *but also* now his ideological or theological partner. Again, the modifying expressions "in the flesh" and "in [the] lord" can be taken as modifiers for *either* Onesimus's return and presence *or* the "brotherhood" between Onesimus and Philemon.

If, indeed, Paul is reconciling estranged brothers, some elements of Philemon make much more general sense. According to Deuteronomy 25, it is a violation of Jewish law to return an escaped slave. Paul was not beyond acting in ways that differed from biblical law, particularly in light of his decision to become a Jesus follower; we also should not assume that liturgical or daily practices among Jews in the first century were uniform. Yet, it is worthwhile to note that according to the "standard reading" of Philemon, Paul would indeed be acting in violation of Deuteronomy *and that he would be doing so without comment*. Paul writes vigorously that he does not advocate the abolition of Jewish law in Romans (e.g. Rom. 3.31; 7.12, 22; 9.6–7), presumably in response to accusations by his opponents. It is not at all unreasonable to presume that Paul would have imagined some comment upon his practice in his letter to Philemon if he were indeed returning an escaped slave to service. It seems striking that he does not address this question. Paul certainly makes a point in his letter to the Galatians to justify his understanding through a different reading of Hebrew Scriptures; using allegory and other interpretive techniques, Paul rethinks and argues in Galatians 4, for example, that Abraham's son Isaac is the "child of slavery" and not, as Genesis 22 asserts, the child promised by God (Martyn 1997: 431–66).

Those who follow the "standard reading" of Philemon might surmise that Paul knew full well that returning an escaped slave to his owner was not consistent with the biblical text, but he did not know how to argue that it was. He remained silent in his letter to Philemon, therefore, hoping that no one would bring it up. It becomes a bit more difficult to imagine that no one involved—Philemon, Archippus, Apphia, the congregation (the Colossians?) or even Onesimus himself—was aware of Deuteronomy or any Jewish practice upon which it is based. Other Jews in antiquity (broadly defined) did address the implications of Deuteronomy 25 and slaveholding, both among Jews and with the general, Gentile populace that surrounded them. Foregrounded in their Jewish identity, holiday celebrations (particularly Passover) and weekly Sabbath practices was God's liberation of them as a formerly enslaved people. Liberation from slavery seemed to have fueled much of the Palestinian Jewish resistance against Rome (Frilingos 2000). Issues of slavery, manumission, and the ethical treatment of slaves were present in the daily lives and the literature of Paul's contemporary Jews (Petersen 1985). There was a strong trend toward caring for slaves in the sex industry, including attempts to secure their liberty (Barclay 1991; Horsley 1998; Byron 2004; Glancy 2006).

Indeed, one can conjecture, infer, or surmise about Onesimus's identity for days. The assumption about Onesimus's slave status is, in the end, simply too equivocal; it is certainly not *prima facie* obvious or clear. The needs, desires, and expectations of the interpreter play an important— perhaps the critical—role in shaping what the interpreter sees as "obvious" and "clear," or which assumptions he or she deems to be more reasonable than others.

Paul's letters often include a thanksgiving prayer that outlines the letter's main themes and concerns. The thanksgiving prayer in Philemon does not stress the language of slavery, the non-assertion of legal rights or the willingness to endure financial loss for the sake of Christian faith (though, it does stress service to and labor for others and it references Paul's incarceration). Primarily, Paul's thanksgiving prayer in Philemon lays out themes of love, acceptance, collaboration, and camaraderie. These emphases would be consistent with a letter that focuses on reuniting estranged siblings or business associates. Philemon begins and ends with themes of confinement and labor, as well as those of family and love.

Reading Philemon and the master class

Noting how assumptions play a role in one's reading of Philemon and how scholars often find themselves convinced by "obvious" moral positions or interpretations, let us return to our earlier question regarding the persuasiveness of Chrysostom's interpretation of Philemon. Why has Chrysostom's reconstruction been taken as "necessary" and "obvious" by so many commentators who are also critical of other options as "conjectural" and "hypothetical?" In many ways, Chrysostom's reading reflects the dominant worldview and assumptions of the literate, commentary-producing, Bible-reading classes.

One reason Chrysostom's reading seems obvious is its long tradition, despite the fact that Chrysostom lived several centuries after Paul. In a real sense, no one reads the Bible for the first time or without commentary. The Bible (still) pervades Western culture, leaving its mark on countless cultural tropes, memes, expressions, and art forms (Edwards 2015). The reading of Philemon inherited by scholars since Chrysostom is the reading upon which most "cut their teeth"; it is the early interpretation that becomes almost impossible to set aside completely. Moving beyond academic scholarship, this reading permeates popular culture, appearing in several mid-century examples of devotional literature and in multiple "sword and sandal" Bible epics in the golden age of cinema (Kreitzer 2008: 107–46, 149–68). For example, Onesimus appears in Norman Walker's British film *The Life of St. Paul* (1938) and occupies the center stage in Yassen Esmail Yassen's Arabic film *The Runaway* (2006). Both these films are intentionally proselytizing.

A second reason, one must grant, is its general persuasiveness. The reading elegantly accounts for most of the data, both internal and external to the letter. As this present monograph exemplifies, it is *very* hard to read or think about the Letter to Philemon and *not* think about slavery. The letter foregrounds servitude, obligation, and labor. Slavery was an integral part of the ancient Roman world. Surely, it is odd that Paul would feel free to comment upon marriage, sex, and employment, but decided that it was socially improper to comment upon slavery. However, his other letters seem to indicate that he actually didn't oppose slavery but saw it as a normal part of society. The implicit endorsement of slavery in Philemon is, then, not inconsistent with Paul's other letters; indeed, the subtle restriction upon slavery identified by Chrysostom would be the aberration. In other words, Chrysostom's reading is consistent with the letter's Greco-Roman context.

Chrysostom's reading also helps explain the internal elements of the letter, including the name "Onesimus," the allusion to slavery, the suggestion of monetary damages and restitution, Onesimus's return and Paul's request. It reasonably identifies the characters named, and traces a vaguely plausible scenario (at least in its skeletal form, even if some of the particulars are a bit strained). Surely, Chrysostom's reading is widely accepted because it "works."

Commentators often point to the history of ancient slaves, their negligence, their tendency to damage property or revolt. These emphases reveal the commentators' assumptions about ancient slaves. Though they can easily claim support from the regular trope of the lazy or treacherous slave in literature and drama from the ancient world (cf. Wills 1998), they fail to acknowledge that these ancient texts often reflect only the views of the master class. Active, even affective, selfless labor by the slave was seen as the master's right. Modern scholars are often ready to apologize for the gruesome reality of slavery in ancient Rome; they are quick to suggest that most ancient slaves didn't have it so bad, and that many who did were themselves pretty lazy. These observations betray a particular social context; readers' identification with the authority of the "master class," in the end, makes Chrysostom's assumptions about Philemon seem "obvious."

Chrysostom's reading of Philemon, though plausible and satisfying, is also based upon substantial speculation and imagination. It has been broadly accepted because it is compelling; yet, several equally compelling narratives could be drawn. Why was *this* argument so compelling? Why did the search for plausible contexts behind Philemon essentially stop with Chrysostom?

A possible answer to this question emerges when we look at the precise moments when Chrysostom's reading becomes unstable. For example, in the antebellum American biblical scholarship of the nineteenth century, Philemon was a flashpoint of controversy (Harrell 2000; Kreitzer 2008: 90–106). For many, it provided biblical endorsement of slavery (Paul does not condemn the institution, ergo it cannot be sinful) and of the controversial Fugitive Slave Act of 1850. This latter was particularly onerous, as it meant that slavery would persist even in states that had laws opposing it. Not only did a southern slave remain a slave when in a northern state, federal law required northern citizens to arrest and return any fugitive slave they might encounter, forcing them to also participate in and perpetuate the institution of slavery. In this context, debates over Philemon raged.

The core question of the nineteenth-century debates over Philemon was v. 16 (cf. Kreitzer 2008; Avalos 2011). Slavery-supporting commentators argued that Paul's letter to Philemon was obvious and clear in its endorsement of slavery; such biblical clarity, according to them, compelled one to admit slavery as a moral rather than an evil institution. Some scholars expressed a sense of labored but sincere compulsion; though they did not like slavery themselves, the Bible forced them to concede it.

However, some abolitionists argued that the letter to Philemon never said that Onesimus was an escaped slave. According to them, readings that assumed Onesimus's slave status were "strained" or conjectural. Some abolitionists, while conceding that Onesimus was a fugitive slave and that Paul did not condemn slavery, countered that Paul was culturally bound; surely, they proposed, Paul would have acted and argued differently if he, like the abolitionists in nineteenth-century America, were in an enlightened representative democracy facing colonial chattel slavery. These views were dismissed by supporters of slavery as wishful thinking or intentional subversion of "clear" and "certain" scriptural truths.

Others suggested that even if the Bible did not condemn slavery, it did not require slavery's perpetuation. This ultimately became the majority view, but one must note that it did so only after slavery became illegal in America. A final few argued that the Bible be abandoned entirely as the basis for democratic law or simply that the Bible was an immoral book. This view represented a minority position, often refuted by accusations that its advocates were outside the traditional Judeo-Christian values upon which America was founded as a nation. Notably, similar points would reoccur in twentieth-century debates about women's rights to vote and to serve as leaders in Christian communities, as well in twenty-first-century debates about marriage equity for those who do not self-identify as heterosexual.

In the context of these debates, the narrative context provided by Chrysostom produced a reading that, for some, no longer fit cultural needs. In other words, Chrysostom's reading was resonant with its readers initially because it met the cultural needs of the time. Chrysostom's narrative emerged from his own cultural moment and satisfied a cultural need: namely, to perpetuate the social and economic necessity of slavery, as well as to provide an ethical counterweight to restrict sexual and violent behavior to or with slaves (or, more realistically, forcing such behavior underground). As social norms changed and slavery itself was no longer understood as ethically viable, Chrysostom's reading, which (re)constructed Paul as one who endorsed slavery, was seen for what it was—a culturally produced system of assumptions and interpretations. These were taken at face value for centuries because, quite simply, they "worked," especially with cultural elites who found resonance with this reading.

Perhaps many of us are already familiar with the concept of heteronormativity. Essentially, what the culture presents as "normal" has been, for centuries, heterosexuality. Its opposite, homosexuality, was deemed deviant and, in some extremes, dysfunctional. Individuals are assumed to be heterosexual unless noted otherwise; as a result, expressions or articulations of heterosexual behavior are rarely, if at all, noted as such. Similar dynamics happen in terms of race. In media, for example, "whiteness" is assumed, so only dark-skinned models or protagonists are surprising and hence noteworthy. Both of these examples are articulations of what our culture has established in literature, media, art, and law as "normal"; identity is always already assumed as white, male, and straight. As expectations about sexual norms, gender identities, and racial attitudes change, "normative" examples are seen for the social constructions and assumptions that they are.

Chrysostom identified with the "master class" of his time in the social conflicts over slavery. In doing so, he was arguably not acting radically different than Paul, regardless of whether Onesimus was literally a slave. Paul in his letter to Philemon identifies more with the master (*kurios*) than with the slave (*dulos*). Likewise, Chrysostom's reading of Philemon reflects his and his culture's own "kurio-normativity." The central figures in his reading are Paul and Philemon; Onesimus vanishes. Like one of Alfred Hitchcock's McGuffin characters, Onesimus is as absent and insignificant as he is essential and central. The same is true of slave (or manual or service) labor. Slavery is the erasure of one's presence and one's humanity. Slave labor and service workers are rarely visible. Many cultures go to great lengths to make them even less so, often even concealing the places they work or closeting their tools and supplies. Slaves and service workers must not be intrusive. Only the effect of their labor, but not its process, can be evident. Onesimus, appropriately, vanishes.

Scholars who assume Onesimus's slave status have for generations regarded Onesimus as disobedient, shiftless, and cagey before meeting Paul. His "crime"? Running away from forced servitude. To put the matter plainly, why is it at all unjust, immoral or criminal to run away from a kidnapper, who violently restrains you and forces you to work? Indeed, wouldn't we try to do the same, even if our kidnapper were "kind" to us? The physical abuse heaped upon slaves was more than simply disciplinary beating. Abuse was one way to remind slaves daily that their very body was not their own. Even if one assumes, despite available evidence, that no form of sexual assault, overture, or impropriety ever took place against a slave, a slave still lost control of her/his own body by being forced to use it in the service of someone else's need and pleasure. The slave body existed solely for the pleasure of someone else; this included its need to work constantly to lighten someone else's workload. More often than not, as we have discussed, this was a situation permeated with sexual and psychological abuse as well. To be anything but wildly sympathetic with Onesimus and to regard his return to his owner with anything but horror is to be inundated and collaborated with the assumptions of kurio-normativity. Chrysostom's reading was considered compelling for centuries because it is a kurio-normative reading that resonated with the dominant class, the very class from which most scholars and commentators emerged (and, certainly, the class which paid for and governed those scholars).

Resisting Chrysostom and the "master class"

The power of kurio-normativity does not, however, go unchallenged. In antebellum America, both the reconstructed context for and the interpretation of Philemon were contested. As Larry Morrison (1980–81: 19) notes: "As far as the New Testament was concerned, the major passage Southerners found which accepted, indeed justified slavery, was the Epistle of St. Paul to Philemon, sometimes referred to as the Pauline Mandate."

In the 1840s, the Reverend Charles Colcock Jones, a Presbyterian missionary to African slaves in the American South and a graduate of Andover and Princeton Seminary, wrote a report to his sponsoring society, describing reaction to a sermon he preached on Philemon to a slave community in 1846. He reports:

> Allow me to relate a fact which occurred in the spring of this year, illustrative of the character and knowledge of negroes at this time. I was preaching to a large congregation on the *Epistle to Philemon*; and when I insisted upon fidelity and obedience as Christian virtues in servants, and, upon the authority of Paul, condemned the practice of *running away*, one half of my audience deliberately rose up and walked off with themselves, and those that remained looked anything but satisfied, either with the preacher or his doctrine. After dismission, there was not a small stir among them: some solemnly declared

that there was no such epistle in the Bible; others, that it was not the [g]ospel; others, that I preached to please masters; others, that they did not care if they ever heard me preach again. (Cited in Callahan 1997: 1)

Callahan notes how the slaves disregarded the authority of both preacher and text, reacting against the grain of kurio-normative reconstruction of history and interpretation of Philemon. For these slaves, something was wrong, whether that was this preacher's reading of the Bible, the morals of the preacher, or the biblical text itself. According to Callahan (1997: 1):

With their own indigenous hermeneutic of suspicion, African American slaves questioned both the authorship and the theological import of Paul's epistle to Philemon ... The slaves themselves brought a radical critique to the purported apostolic sanction of slavery.

This episode reported by Colcock Jones shows how "unlearned" slaves rejected his reading because they didn't like its outcome or implication. Certainly, rejection of either the "obvious" interpretation or application of Philemon was "not permissible" for many educated whites. Nor was it, however, tolerable to many enslaved listeners in Colcock Jones's audience. Tellingly, they rebelled by "walking off with themselves."

We could, however, reframe Colcock Jones as well as his reading and preaching. These "unlearned" slaves had not been indoctrinated into kurio-normative standards and could not escape the ethical challenges inherent in slave systems and their active perpetuation. Slaves reading from their own location were, of course, considered by people like Colcock Jones to be less critical or "unlearned"; unlike the "standard reading," slave reading was the supplanting reason for personal interests. Notably though, observing how "learned" interpretations of Philemon reinforced social structures that were favorable to the class of "learned" white exegetes did not seem to work equally to suggest that the "standard reading" was also the subordinating reason for personal or class-based advantages. The slave audience, though "unlearned," was actually very correct; Colcock Jones's reading was inundated with assumptions and conjectures. His sermon, as evidenced by his selection of text, selective reading, and condescending report, was permeated with language and argument that we would recognize today as racist.

Reorientation away from kurio-normative readings also awakens attention to the assumptions inherent in Chrysostom's narrative. Reading the text very closely, Callahan reconstructs a very different backstory for Philemon. Drawing upon Paul's encouragement to love and to accept as well as honing in on the ambivalent modifier of v.16 ("in flesh and in lord"), Callahan argues that Onesimus was, indeed, being sent along with Paul's delegation to carry Paul's letter to the Colossians to its audience. Paul was aware that Philemon, Onesimus's *brother*, lived in the area of Colossae and that the two had, in the past, quarreled. Paul wrote, therefore, a second letter, endorsing and recommending Onesimus and encouraging a reconciliation between the brothers.

Callahan is not, however, shy about treating the issue of slavery and the question of Philemon's role in its perpetuation. For centuries, Philemon was used as a base text to defend slavery and maintain its systems. Callahan draws on vv. 18–19 to reflect on how Paul is aware that debts and damages need to be repaid. Apology is not sufficient; reparations for real damages are needed before equilibrium and full peace can be restored to ruptured relationships. Moral repair, at some level, requires repayment and restitution.

It is difficult to imagine a way to incur greater mass indebtedness than systemic slavery. Slaves, especially but not exclusively the race-based system of slavery found in the modern colonial powers such as America, stripped slaves of identity, home, family, and basic humanity. The tragic irony is that the grand and historic state houses in the south—for example, the State house of Montgomery, Alabama, which actually casts a shadow over Martin Luther King's former congregation—were built by slave labor. Wealth and identity were systematically stripped from generations of people, along with their ability to establish either estate or memory; their inheritors and children were often sold away to other owners. This systematic system of theft and social murder was occurring while the owners were enriching themselves by the forced labor of slaves. At the time of the American Civil War, slaves in the south represented a greater collection of wealth than any other asset in the national economy; productivity of slave labor in agricultural markets, matched with historically low (and southern set) tariffs, made the American South a world leader in exports. Astonishing and unprecedented wealth was therefore amassed in a few southern estates. Slavery was big business, and it was a business founded upon the theft of assets and labor of an entire class of fellow humans. Slavery was theft and murder on massive scale.

Given his letter's long association with the perpetuation of slavery, Paul's remark to Philemon about "making good" on damages (vv. 18–19) awakens a real, modern ethical question. African Americans remain unremitted for this damage to their wealth and labor. Consistently and disproportionately impoverished, the legacy of slavery (with the subsequent systems of racial segregation and discrimination) continues to victimize generations of African Americans. Callahan raises this question acutely and actively. Modern readers may shake their heads in wonder about how powerful classes in nineteenth-century America could so readily use their education, resources and power to at least tolerate, if not perpetuate, slavery. Yet, the question of reparations still remains largely submerged.

Conclusion

Chrysostom's narrative of an escaped slave being returned certainly *can* be a way of reading Philemon, but it is replete with questionable assumptions, imaginary history, and problematic implications. What assumptions or imagination are compelling to a reader or interpreter is always, in part, a result of the reader's social location and needs. For Chrysostom, and for generations of readers, the need was control and perpetuation of slave systems. But Chrysostom's is not the only way, or necessarily the most satisfying. Paul's letter to Philemon can be reread. We are not compelled to read Philemon this way. We have chosen to; we may choose not to as well. Most of all, we need to be aware of the assumptions, historical imagination, and current interests that *we* are bringing to our reading. For later readers, for instance, the concern may be the maintenance of a "moral" reading of Paul and his canonized texts.

Reading Philemon with a critical eye toward the "obvious" interpretation of Chrysostom reveals how often assumptions and historical imagination are at work behind the scene, how critical these are to the interpretation, and how they betray the investments of the interpreter. It is challenging to ask why this particular set of assumptions and why this particular imaginary context are preferred. When we look at circumstances in which this reading *is not* preferred, we find them among those reading from outside the "master class" and kurio-normativity, suggesting that what makes Chrysostom "compelling" and "obvious" is very likely more the way it assists perpetuation of power structures than its inherent appeal.

4

Labor and Love: An Affect Reading of Philemon

Reconstructing a stable background or context for the interpretation of Philemon, as we have seen, has proven more difficult than we first imagined. Going further into various questions on the interpretation of Philemon and its potential contexts provides an opportunity to examine how scholarship on the letter not only intersects with traditional questions about the most staid of historical approaches to New Testament reading such as authorship, canon, and text, but also offers opportunity to reread Philemon with more innovative strategies of reading. This chapter will develop along these latter and later lines. What we will find is that, while Philemon continues to resist attempts to identify a definitive, final meaning intended by its ancient author, it is remarkably fertile for constructing an array of possible meanings that is relevant to contemporary readers both inside and outside Christian confessional traditions.

Erasing Paul: F. C. Baur and a pseudepigraphic Philemon

New Testament scholarship of the past two hundred years, particularly scholarship with an eye toward history, has presented challenges and questions to traditional readings of the Pauline writings. Scholars of both the New Testament and early Christianity have noted that a number of early Christian writings that circulated throughout antiquity make false claims about authorship. These writings are termed "pseudepigraphic" ("false author" or "false title"). More cynically, one might refer to them as "forgery" (Ehrman 2013).

Forged letters and lost letters

As we noted earlier, within the New Testament itself, questions regarding Pauline authorship have legitimately been raised. Paul expresses concern to the Galatians that they not heed any reports bearing a "new gospel," whether from outsiders or from Paul himself (Gal. 1.8). The latter concern suggests a fear of letters being falsely circulated in Paul's name (cf. 2 Thess. 2.1–2). This concern is perhaps also behind occasional assertions that "Paul" is writing "in his own hand" (2 Thess. 3.17; cf. 1 Cor. 16.21; Gal. 6.11; Col. 4.18). Clearly, someone in the ancient community knew that false letters might circulate.

This concern does not seem idle or unfounded. As we saw in the Introduction, there are references within the Pauline writings to letters which no longer exist: a letter to the Laodiceans (Col. 4.16), an earlier letter to the Corinthians before 1 Corinthians (1 Cor. 5.9) and another "angry letter" to the Corinthians written between the canonical 1 and 2 Corinthians (2 Cor. 2.3–4; 7.8). Within the surviving corpus of early Christian writings, we indeed find ancient letters not only titled "To the Laodiceans" and "3 Corinthians" but also others claiming Pauline authorship. The canonical Pauline collection does not contain everything Paul wrote, but neither did Paul write everything contained within the canonical Pauline collection.

It remains to be argued whether or not these are "forgeries" (someone attempting to use the name of a more notable leader to substantiate an argument) or attempted homage (a student taking on the voice of a revered master to address later concerns). Both options have been posited and are possible. Also, perhaps these letters were never intended to circulate; perhaps an ecstatic Christian follower became convinced that the spirit of a former leader now resided within her/him, and the follower wrote a letter down just for herself/himself. Whatever motive one might speculate and attribute to these letter writers, one must face the practical reality that not all authorial claims for early Christian literature are genuine.

If there are writings falsely claiming Pauline authorship, then could some of the canonical letters also be pseudepigraphic? Indeed, Bart Ehrman (2013) has noted that the vast majority of extant early Christian writing circulated anonymously (with authorship being assigned by later, perhaps erroneous, Christian tradition) or pseudepigraphically. He suggests, in fact, that the burden of proof lies upon the more irregular and difficult claim of explicitly named authorship (1, 5). Attempts to ascertain authorship claims are complex because we don't have access to all the data, and much of what we have, like Philemon, is too brief for definitive analysis. There is little information on who first collected the letters of Paul into a group. We can presume that the motive was admiration for Paul and his teaching. We don't know, however, what resources the collector(s) had, if the collection contained any additional edits, how letters were initially evaluated and selected or what, if any, letters were rejected or simply missing. The letters we read today are also fossil-like reconstructions of long lost originals. We do not have the original copy (the "autograph") of any New Testament writing. Among our most ancient copies are second-century fragments written on papyri; among these is a portion of Philemon (Parker 2008: 249–55).

Philemon's authenticity and canonization

The history of including Philemon in a group or a canon of Paul's writings is curious. The earliest list of a "canonical" collection of Paul is that of the Roman bishop Marcion, who was later regarded as a heretic. Marcion only accepted the Pauline writings (without the Pastorals) and Luke-Acts, rejecting the Hebrew Bible entirely. His collection does not mention Philemon; in its place is the letter to the "Laodiceans." Many scholars consider "Laodiceans" Marcion's title for Philemon, but his collection actually does not include any other personal letters; the Pastorals (1 Timothy, 2 Timothy, and Titus), as I mentioned, are missing.

Certainly, writers prior to Marcion considered some writings as sacred (normally the Jewish Scriptures); they also read and recommended the reading of others now regarded as Christian. The author of 2 Peter, for example, knows of Pauline letters (2 Pet. 3.15–16), as does Clement and very likely also Ignatius, though none of these writers (or any others) clearly regard Paul's writings as equal or superior to the stature of the Hebrew Bible (Metzger 1987: 42–43). Nor do they offer a definitive list of "approved" books.

Among the earliest writers to cite Philemon is Tertullian (an ancient writer who, rather famously, disliked Paul as the "Apostle to the Heretics"), and Philemon appears to have been regarded as authoritative by Tertullian's time. Tertullian claims that Marcion also knew Philemon (*Adv. Marc.* 5.21). Philemon was known by Origen, who thought it Pauline (*Hom on Jer* 19); it is also listed in the Muratorian Canon. Since the third century, Philemon's authenticity and authority, unlike its significance, have largely not been debated.

We see therefore, despite its relative brevity and simplicity, Philemon figures prominently in very interesting scholarly work on the antiquity and the integrity of the New Testament manuscripts, in discussion of the earliest collection(s) of the Pauline writings and in the search for the earliest "canon lists" of approved and recommended writings. While we don't know who first collected and preserved the collection of Pauline writings, we have mentioned in Chapter 3 how Knox and Goodenough argued that (1) Onesimus was instrumental in, if not instigating, this process; and (2) the letter to Philemon was critical to the collection (Goodenough 1929; Knox 1959). What I would like to emphasize now is how the preservation of ancient documents, the hand copying of handwritten copies, the careful collection and review of any variant readings, the painstaking reconstruction of a likely original draft from those variants and the deliberate editing all involve exacting and anonymous labors. Similar labors are involved in attempts to authenticate authorship.

Ancient writings did not have colophons or copyright symbols. To establish authenticity and legitimacy of authorship, scholars examine them, looking for telltale marks of consistency or variation. Scholars look for common and consistent vocabulary and style, similar conceptual understandings, general historical veracity, and other factors. Markers of genuine authorship are often vocabulary, characteristic style, identifiable referents or contexts, theology, and mode of argumentation. Scholars also consider external elements, such as associated literature, quotation by early church leaders, canonical lists (cf. Seesengood 2010: 20–56). Though the vast majority of contemporary scholarship on Philemon accepts Pauline authorship, the question is actually far from certain, especially if one takes a closer look again at these evaluative markers.

Though the voice of Philemon is generally consistent with the other six so-called undisputed letters of Paul, Philemon contains a substantial number of words used only once in these Pauline letters and in the New Testament. While Paul's characteristic love of wordplay or punning is present, the grammar, vocabulary, and style of Philemon deviate from the undisputed letters *more than the Pastoral letters do*. If one examines the grammar and vocabulary of Philemon very closely, they seem idiosyncratic to and different from the Paul we know from his other letters. This would suggest concern regarding Philemon's authorship.

The letter of Philemon is also an unusual format for Paul. In his other letters, Paul writes to an entire community. His letters are also rather long. In Philemon, we find a remarkably short document addressed primarily to a single individual. Philemon deviates from the form and style of the other undisputed Pauline letters. The recipients' names in Philemon are largely unknown. Paul's associates named in the letter's conclusions are known, but they are only known through later traditions (such as Acts of the Apostles) and in documents also with debated authorship (such as Colossians). Beyond Philemon and Colossians, there is no evidence of Paul having ministered in or having connections with any church at Colossae.

Philemon is very often associated with Colossians, whose authorship is still being questioned. Colossians, somewhat famously, shares several similar or overlapping parts with Ephesians. There are also concerns about the Christology of Colossians; perhaps the central debate surrounds whether or not Colossians suggests a notion of Jesus's divinity that, in its clarity of expression if not its content, is too late for Paul. The theology of Philemon also deviates in interesting ways from other undisputed letters by Paul. If Onesimus was a slave and Paul in Philemon appeals for Onesimus's freedom, why does Paul tell slaves in 1 Cor. 7.21–24 not to seek out their own freedom?

In Philemon Paul refers to himself as either an "old man" or an ambassador (v. 9), presumably of Jesus (cf. Birdsall 1993). Nowhere else does he use either title in the other undisputed letters. Overseer or "elder" is an office reflected in later Christian congregational polity (cf. 1 Timothy 2 and its parallel in Titus). In addition, traditions surrounding Paul's death suggest that he was not likely to have lived far beyond middle age. Paul also refers to himself as a "prisoner of Christ" (v. 9). This is not his normal way of identifying or describing himself; he never calls himself an "apostle" in Philemon, as he tends to do in his other letters (e.g. Rom. 1.1; 1 Cor. 1.1; Gal. 1.1; 1 Thess. 2.7). Though many suggest that Paul was incarcerated in Ephesus at the writing of Philemon (e.g. Lightfoot 1916; Lohse 1971; Bruce 1984; Coursar 2009), there is no record in Paul's letters or in Acts of his incarceration in Ephesus beyond a cryptic reference in 1 Cor. 15.32. Of course, Paul also refers to himself in Philemon as Onesimus's father, as Apphia's brother, as Archippus's fellow-in-arms and claims to have saved Philemon's life (vv. 2, 10, 19); clearly, Paul uses metaphor and he might not actually be incarcerated when he wrote Philemon.

If we turn to external use or citation of Philemon, while we find little dispute among early Christian writers regarding Paul's authorship, we also find very little interest in the epistle at all. Theordore of Mopsuestia defends Pauline authorship of the letter, but doesn't really clarify who (if anyone) would oppose the idea and seems to indicate a lack of interest in Philemon generally (*Ep. Ad Phlm.* 2.259–60). There are very few early church leaders quoting from Philemon, and the majority are from the fourth century after

Chrysostom. Earliest witnesses suggest that many found Philemon problematic or trivial. It was not consistently named in canonical lists prior to Chrysostom and Jerome's later inclusion of Philemon in his Vulgate. Jerome's preface for Philemon there (*Ep. Ad. Phlm. Prolg.*) repeats Chrysostom's hypothesis and argues for Philemon's legitimate place in the canon despite claims of its insignificance. Christian scholarship's position on Philemon is largely unchanged since Jerome, so there have been no sustained debates about either Philemon's inclusion or significance afterward. This seems inconclusive, though, as we've noted, Jerome's argument is late and fairly conjectural, and questions about pseudepigraphy are generally dismissed by identifying the alternatives as also conjectural and then making an appeal to "tradition." Tradition is used to defend the legitimacy of tradition.

As we have seen, Philemon imitates the "benefactor's letter of appeal" found from ancient worthies such as Pliny. It would not be unusual for later Christian writers to have created Philemon simply to make sure that the Pauline corpus includes a letter of this type. In many ways, the model of Seneca's "belles lettres" or "beautiful-writing" collection serves as a paradigm for the Pauline corpus, especially since Paul was, if nothing else, the paradigmatic social patron (the *amicus domini*) for many early Christians. In classical traditions, several authors (such as Herodotus, Xenophon, Cicero, and Seneca) frame moral and general essays as letters or letter collections. These "letters," though having all the structural marks of an epistle and being addressed to an individual, are clearly documents written for broader, public consumption. These collections developed, over time, into a genre of collected types and clichéd exemplars. One particular type or set piece was an appeal on behalf of a subordinate. The letters were often demonstrations of the patron's rhetorical skill, generosity, and care for the socially inferior— that is, the patron's benevolence. Someone could well have perceived the existing letters of Paul as lacking or needing a letter of this type. Clearly the conceit of collected letters was common among Paul's intellectual contemporaries (some ancient community even forged a correspondence between Paul and Seneca). It would not be unimaginable for a later forger or student to craft a letter of reference—modeled after Pliny's?—to round out the Pauline corpus.

For these and other reasons, F. C. Baur argued in the nineteenth century that Philemon was not really written by Paul. Baur's arguments are often mentioned by modern commentators, only to be quickly dismissed without much reason or explanation. Perhaps there are more questions and observations than arguments in Baur, one must admit. Rebuttal against Baur has, therefore, no clear target, and the data pool (i.e. the word count) of Philemon is tauntingly small. Surely, none of the factors I have described above conclusively argue against Paul as the author of Philemon. Yet, they do stand unrefuted and, in many ways, irrefutable. These factors, taken together, suggest at least as much suspicion about the authorship of Philemon as is warranted for Ephesians, Colossians, and 2 Thessalonians. There is just as much reason to challenge Pauline authorship of Philemon as there is to challenge Colossians or 2 Thessalonians. Indeed, I think there is more. One wonders if scholars haven't considered the question largely because they see less theological merit or value in Philemon.

It is possible that Philemon made it into the canon largely because it carried the name of Paul and was deemed, frankly, too theologically insignificant to bother with elaborate arguments for or against its inclusion. In many ways, it may continue to find its Pauline authorship undisputed for exactly the same reasons. No one really cares enough to challenge Philemon seriously. The disinterest that once led to Philemon's inclusion in the canon may also be the very thing that has spared it from close historical scrutiny. The lack of scrutiny may be exactly what has allowed Chrysostom's reading to stand. But is Philemon too trivial or too bound up in defunct ancient culture and mores to reward contemporary, close reading?

A letter without origin or ending

Our readings so far have focused on the triad of Paul, Onesimus, and Philemon. In readings that emphasize Onesimus's slave status, Onesimus is effectively erased. At best "useful," his actual interests, desires, and needs are inconsequential. Paul (perhaps?) hints at a desire for Onesimus's freedom not because Onesimus's humanity demands it or because Onesimus seems to want it; Paul's request is so that Onesimus can continue to serve Paul as, in Paul's interpretation, a service of the gospel; we might also note that Paul says that *he* personally thinks a great deal of Onesimus. When the context of Philemon is read in ways that see Onesimus as an estranged slave, Onesimus is erased.

In readings that do not see Onesimus as the escaped slave of Philemon (e.g. Knox 1955; Elliott 2011), Philemon is diminished. Indeed, in Knox's reading, Philemon is not even the letter's recipient. In readings that go further and do not even see strong arguments that Onesimus is a slave at all (e.g. Callahan 1997), the attention of readers turns away from Philemon.

We realize through those readings how much we have been inclined toward seeing Philemon as integral because of kurio-normative ways of reading. Foregrounding Onesimus encourages us to reexamine the ethics of keeping Philemon prominent.

But what happens when we read the letter to Philemon without Paul? How does removing Paul from the triad affect the letter? In many ways, Philemon becomes "groundless" and "context-less" once again, even though the excision of Paul from the letter can only occur after we have burrowed and dug into the history of Philemon within the ancient literary and cultural context of nascent Christianity.

Much has been made of reading and interpretive strategies since Roland Barthes's (1968) work on the "death of the author." Readers create meaning from texts. What authors intend is irrelevant. Certainly, pseudepigraphy is the ultimate erasure of the author, but does it also erase textual meaning? Does it mean readers are free to interpret as they will? Within biblical studies, poststructuralist readings indebted to critics like Barthes are often set in sharp contrast to readings that are rigorously steeped in historical and grammatical analysis. Ironically, like all pseudepigraphic arguments, Philemon may be viewed as "author-less" precisely because of our consideration of its canonization history and reconstructed context(s). Erasing an author does not necessarily unmoor a writing completely from context or history. Indeed, the removal of Paul from Philemon reinforces analysis of historical and literary context. Philemon presents the challenge of having too many potentially apt contexts, all of which can be plausibly reconstructed. We cannot reconstruct the historical setting for Philemon because it is, in some ways, too fertile. The same is true of its canonization history; we can just as easily argue that it got into the canon not because Paul composed it, but because of a desire to compose a certain picture of Paul by Paul's followers.

Barthes, who was in many ways simply finishing lines first drawn by Friedrich Nietzsche, problematizes interpretations which are dependent upon our certainty about an author's intention or even identity. Julia Kristeva (1980) has expanded the argument even more by suggesting that all meaning is "intertextual." That is to say, ideas and experiences from multiple texts and reading worlds, contexts, or communities collide in the encounter of a reader and a text.

These intertextualities become particularly acute with Philemon. Philemon is so short and so context-free—and so much like a scrap of a letter discovered at random in a library—that every reading of it is always already an intertextual reading. If we "must" reconstruct an author's intended meaning for valid interpretation, then we are incapacitated by Philemon, since we can't even clearly decide to whom the letter is written, let alone for what purpose. While modern commentators assert that "there is no reason to challenge authorship," they do not actually mount arguments to defend that assertion. Even if one argues in favor of Paul's authorship (which is, in my view, far from settled), one must admit that the resulting assertions of authorship are only marginally useful. Philemon is too short to argue definitively and finally either for or against Paul's authorship or a particular context or background. Given the possibility for different reconstructions and interpretations, Philemon, more than revealing *a* reading or meaning, offers the potential to examine reading or textual meaning itself.

Aside from challenges to the ethics of biblical interpretation presented by the assumption of Onesimus's slave status (whether or not Paul, Paul's interpreters, or both miss a cue for not recognizing the inherent immorality of slavery), Philemon challenges systems of interpretation that rely upon historicity or upon authorial identity and context. If we cannot legitimately read Philemon without reconstructing the original context, can we legitimately read Philemon? As we have seen, we can adduce no clear, final argument about either the letter's recipient(s) or the topic(s). Indeed, one could argue (as I have above) that we also cannot be certain about its authorship.

What, then, do we do with a letter that lacks audience, topic, and now even author? What kind of reading emerges from Philemon if we consider the letter without Paul or without a reconstructed context? What happens when we are reading the Bible without any notion of author, context, or even a clear, singular negotiated space of social exchange? Reading without authors is reading with and in community: the reading of text, the reading of continuity, the reading of implication. It is the reading of reading itself. It is the reading of commentaries and interpretations. It is, to borrow words from Philemon, the reading of "fellowship" or *koinōnia* (v. 6).

Affect theory and Philemon: Emotional labor and invisible slaves

Philemon certainly understands "fellowship" and community. Indeed, it is a letter filled with feelings, bonds, relationships, including those that are estranged, newly knit or newly built. Paul refers to Philemon as a "dear friend" (v. 1). Apphia is a "sister," and Archippus a "comrade in arms" (v. 2). Paul bids them God's grace and peace (v. 3). Paul is prayerfully grateful for Philemon's love toward others (v. 5) and for Philemon's own recognition of the good that he can bring about as a follower of Christ (v. 6). This love brings Paul joy (v. 7). Paul appeals in love to Philemon (v. 9) for his "child" Onesimus (v. 10), Paul's "very heart" (v. 12). "Heart" as the translation for *splagchna* is a typical English convention, but this is a dynamic, not literal, translation. *Splagchna* refers to kidneys or bowels. In Greek convention, these were the source of one's deepest, innermost emotions (somewhat comparable to say in English, "to feel it in one's gut"). As per Koine Greek convention, *splagchna* refers to inner and intensely felt emotions or even to one's innermost self.

The appeal to Philemon is also deferentially made to his kindness (v. 14) and on behalf of a "dear brother" (v. 16). Paul urges reconciliation (vv. 17–19) by his dear "brother" (v. 20), in whom he is fully confident (v. 21). In other words, the letter to Philemon oozes with the language of emotion. Love, gratitude, and thanksgiving appear in almost every verse. As I have mentioned in Chapter 1, the very name Philemon ("lover of people" or "affectionate one" in Greek) echoes with "love."

Turning to affects

Beginning within the social sciences with the work of psychologist Silvan Tomkins (1962–92), the language of affect and affect theory is growing as a critical approach in the humanities. Affect is emotional response. Within earliest social science research, affect theory was probing precognitive emotive responses (e.g. disgust, fear, lust, compassion, laughter). Affect is responsive, prerational.

A turn toward examination of human emotion has marked general social science and humanities scholarship of the late twentieth and early twenty-first century (cf. Gregg and Seigworth 2010), including that of biblical studies (cf. Kotrosits 2015: 1–20; Koosed and Moore 2014a). In part, much of this work emerged from scholarly attention to embodiment and subjectivity. Selves are not mere consciousness, mental collections of ideas and concepts; selves are embodied and have feelings and emotions. Affect theory provides a way to bypass debates between humanities scholarship that emphasizes biologically inherent universals (such as essentialism and structuralism) and scholarship that emphasizes culturally learned particularities (such as constructivism and poststructuralism). Its early work focused on disgust, revulsion, desire, lust, and other emotional responses to stimuli that occur before one can even clearly process cognitively what one is seeing or experiencing. Still carrying much of the ideological freight of essentialist debates, affect theory also connects with inquiry into the "posthuman" or the differences among humans, animals, and technologies. Its work is often rooted in queer, gender, and feminist studies, partly because of the emphasis all these place upon embodiment and partly in response to centuries of argument that emotion was less than fully rational or masculine.

Affect criticism first entered humanities discourse principally via literary and film theory. In film studies, for example, affect merges with viewer-response criticism(s) to explore audience reaction to an array of images. In many ways, film, by presenting narrative along with intense visual stimulus and music, is more immediately affectual than print literature. A critical insight of this scholarship is the recognition that emotional engagement with a film is embodied, often "automatic" and not separable as an element of the image's or film's "meaning." Just as the meaning of a film transcends simple script and is communicated via music, lighting, editing, mise-en-scène, and a host of other semiotic elements; its meaning also transcends what is narrative and rational but includes an affective, emotional, responsive element.

In literary criticism affect theory emerges in the work of scholars such as Eve Sedgwick (2011), Sara Ahmed (2004), and others who are exploring the affectual turn in literature. Much of this work, especially the work of Sedgwick, is to provide an intentional corrective to scholarly tendencies to theoretical reification (i.e. the tendency to make a single approach or "theory" the principal means for unpacking communication). In a similar way, affect disrupts various binaries, especially the bifurcation between linguistic and affective/emotive content in discourse.

Affect readings foreground emotions and literature or emotions in literature, particularly in the ways literary or filmic works create or manipulate general "affects." Affect readings pursue these responses, as well as the impulse behind their creation, as an integral part of meaning. Affect theory has more recently entered into religious studies and has been particularly fruitful in providing a supplement or a corrective to different theories of religion, such as Clifford Geertz's view of religion as worldview, Émile Durkheim's or Mircea Eliade's view of religion as social organizer, and Diana Eck's views of religious symbol and ritual. Donovan Schaefer (2015) reimagines religion itself as principally driven by affects and not language and belief. Affect is the precognitive, a form of prerational thinking or instantaneous response. In this line of argument, affect is an "in-between" feeling, an idea in its origins and its becomings. Affect is the instant one sees something disgusting and responds physically and emotively, only later pausing to put rational thoughts and ideas on the experience. It is difficult not to see some level of affect in Durkheim's "Sacred" or Sigmund Freud's "*unheimlich*." Affect, like religion, is a form of prerational, preconscious cognition and knowing.

Within the fields of early Christianity and biblical studies, affect readings are also an emerging trend. Jennifer Koosed and Stephen Moore (2014b) have produced one of the first edited collections of affect-driven work, but it will certainly not be the last given the intense interest in affect—an interest that is readily apparent in conference papers and emerging scholarly literature. Maia Kotrosits (2015) has shown affect to be a particularly useful category for reading early Christian literature in general and ancient apocalyptic literature in particular. Biblical texts inspire emotions; apocalyptic texts repulse, encourage, frighten, inspire, and alienate. Paul's letters are particularly rife with emotions; they seethe with anger at times (e.g. Galatians 1; 2 Corinthians 10) and coo with affection at others (e.g. Galatians 4; 2 Corinthians 2). Paul is obsessed with agape love and authors the Bible's most soaring tribute to love in 1 Corinthians 13. The affective power of Philemon has been noted by more traditional New Testament critics as well (Lampe 2010; cf. Lohse 1971; Barclay 1991).

Emotional labor then and now

As we have seen, Philemon, as an epistle, is filled with the language of emotions and feelings to the degree that it becomes, in places, melodramatic and sentimental. Philemon's very name echoes with "love" (*phileō*). Yet Philemon is also a letter of labor, as implied in Onesimus's name ("useful"). Onesimus, once "useless," is now "useful" and not just in name (v. 11). Alongside its affect is a concern for effectiveness and duty. Philemon is a "*coworker*" (v. 1), but note how the letter ties his love to his faith or faithfulness (v. 5). What the letter applauds is Philemon's love (and faithfulness) toward the "saints" (from the Greek, *hagios*). Accordingly, Philemon's "love" (*agapē*) is not abstract but is active and produces an observable result (v. 7). Paul gives thanks for Philemon (and calls him a "fellow worker" in v. 1) not because of his affective love, but because his love is effective. It achieves a result in and for others: their "hearts" are "refreshed" (*anapepautai*, from *anapauō*), Paul writes in v. 7. *Anapauō* means "to give a release from toil" or "to provide rest from labor." Philemon's love reduces the labor or struggle of the other saints either metaphorically or, perhaps, quite literally (vv. 6–8). The letter speaks of Philemon's "duty" (v. 8). Philemon is being referred to as a partner, which is a word with economic overtones (v. 17). The letter addresses financial matters and debts (vv. 16–20).

The careful and oblique rhetoric throughout the letter is Philemon's compliance, his complete obedience. Note how the rhetoric merges love and duty over and over again. Love, affect, duty, and labor all fuse in Philemon, most visibly in v. 14, where Philemon is asked to comply "out of love" and not merely out of "duty" (cf. v. 8). Note, furthermore, how love and labor are fused in v. 7, where Philemon's love and service to others, particularly his compliance with the requests to receive and release ("refresh") Onesimus from obligation (perhaps labor), also "comforts" (*paraklēsin*) the letter writer. The letter of Philemon is, in these precise moments, equating work and affect. Affect is abundant in Philemon, but it is also effectual: love works. Philemon is a call for emotional labor, for compliance not from "duty" or from command but from genuine "love."

Within the larger study of affect is a conversation on emotional labor. Emotional labor refers to work, largely service-oriented, that involves caretaking or requires the illusion of regard on the part of the service provider. The term, as used by Arlie Hochschild (1983), refers to spheres of service labor dealing with cognitive engagement, body care, forms of intimate service (such as domestic labor of cleaning and cooking) and the assuagement and resolution of grievance. With the industrial revolution, Western employment shifted from largely agrarian work and cottage industries to mass industrial manufacturing. As Western economies change under the pressures of late capitalism and its expansive technologies, employment has moved yet again and become largely based on service. Many of these jobs and occupations involve traditionally feminine, maternal, domestic roles. Sara Ahmed (2010), in her critique of emotional labor and its integration into neoliberal service-based economic systems, notes how standards and productivity expectations of workers often place great affective demands and stresses upon workers even as—or because?—they facilitate economic growth and consumption (Ahmed 2010).

Workers today fill a variety of service roles from sophisticated and highly skilled labor (e.g. mental care, social work, health care, and education) to less skilled tasks (e.g. child or pet care, sanitation and cleaning, food preparation). Relative strangers performing these tasks are actually providing intimate bodily care and addressing intimate bodily needs, though the care and needs may range from the significant (e.g. rehabilitative therapy) to trivial (e.g. haircuts) to luxuriant (e.g. massage). Emotional labor includes not only these forms of work, but also sales and retail, customer service, complaint adjudication and resolution, food service, and similar careers. In these latter forms of emotional labor, workers are required to assuage angry customers and (at least, appear) to care deeply about the satisfaction of customer concerns and worries. Workers must not merely be competent and professional or even courteous (despite often angry and disrespectful clients); they must also *communicate* deep concern for the client and her/his needs.

In fact, substantial research has been conducted regarding the mood and emotional state of customers and how that correlates to perceived satisfaction with a given transaction (or, more to the point, amount of expenditure and return sales). Certainly, the perceived emotional state of a service employee affects a customer's emotional state, yet there remains some doubt as to whether the marketing holy grail of "emotional contagion" (where a service worker can actively, predictably, and fully alter the emotional state of a client) occurs (Hennig-Thurau et al. 2006). Emotional labor takes a very real toll on many workers. Workers are often required to suppress chronic stress. They are often evaluated on their ability to manage or even direct the emotional state and felt-satisfaction of customers and clients, even though it seems increasingly unlikely that they can have any real effect on another person's emotions (cf. Bitner, Booms and Tetrault 1990; Ashforth and Humphrey 1993; Bulan, Erickson and Wharton 1997).

A great deal of contemporary labor involves maintaining an illusion of affective bonds, in part because doing so increases productivity and efficiency (and return sales). This is also partly because this affective illusion is much of what customers are paying to receive. In addition to service, consumers also want love. Consumers want workers who embrace their work joyfully and do more than the "bare minimum"; they want workers who smile, flirt, or flatter to make their transaction a happy one.

Emotional labor is the (post)modern mechanism of culture and productivity of late capitalism. We purchase intimacy in our engagement with service workers. We expect pleasantness from a clerk or waiter, even if (when?) we are ourselves rushed, curt, or rude. Indeed, very often our rudeness or curtness is taken as the fault of the service worker. Emotional labor is supposed to smooth over harshness or awkwardness in commercial exchange for service, particularly service that is intimate. It creates the illusion that service workers *want* to make their clients happy, that they would even provide their service or pleasure to us for free. It is the illusion that enables exploitation. It is late capitalism's mass opiate. A pleasant exchange creates a social fiction whose fuel is the self-direction, inner essence, and dignity of the service worker. Emotional labor enables the grist of the economy to continue. As scholars of emotional labor in late capitalism argue, emotional labor is the residue of increasing economic disparity, where those served are no longer content with the labor and bodies of their workers, but want their emotions as well.

Emotional labor is (intentionally) hidden labor. Service workers are pleasant often because this affords the minimal disruption, because affect affects economic exchanges, particularly in a way that preserves the dignity and status of the customer or employer. But there are also elements of emotional labor expectations among a variety of more professional, culturally empowered careers. Doctors and nurses are expected to demonstrate concern and compassion. Teachers are expected to love their students. Politicians are expected to affectively love their cities or jurisdictions. Professional, stable competency is no longer sufficient; work must reflect "love." But in all these cases, affect can also blind evaluation of real qualifications, actual performance, actual costs (tangible and intangible), and concrete effect.

Emotional labor has been, in part, the hallmark of domestic labor and spiritual labor for eons. Slaves are erased exactly because they are forced into affective engagement with their masters. As we have noted, slaves must serve whether or not they choose to do so. They must feed and care for children, as well as clean homes that are not their own as if they were their own. Slaves and domestic labor prepare and serve food they will never eat. They tend to the wounds and bodies of nonfamily members. They solve the problems of strangers. They touch and groom and dress someone else's body. They do this often while, because of the hours and energy lost, their own food is cold and bland, their own children are neglected, their own homes untended, their own health and bodies uncared for, their own problems unresolved. Despite this, so many still don't comment on instructions, even within the New Testament (e.g. Col. 3.22–23), that slaves are to do all this *and* love their jobs and masters.

Slaves performed their service for free. The service workers of late capitalism must act as if they would perform their service for free as well. Indeed, both slaves and service workers must act as if they *are* doing it because of affection. They often must perform in ways that exceed the demands of the job. The illusion of late capitalism—like slavery—is labor steeped in love.

Emotional labor is hidden labor. That is its very point: emotional labor is the illusion that one is not serving another for the sole purpose of remunerative exchange. It conceals the work involved, and, even more, hides the laborer. Workers recede into the background of the exchange or "experience." They are often actively hidden or intentionally discrete.

Like slaves and slavery.
Like the setting, character and thesis of Philemon.

As we have already seen, the pull toward discounting slave emotions is so strong that, hundreds of years after the composition of Philemon, modern biblical critics still sometimes argue that slaves *liked* their work, *loved* their masters, and often felt superior to freedmen and grateful for their lot. The letter's utter lack of concern for Onesimus's feelings goes very often unremarked (if noticed). Onesimus is praised for no quality other than his "usefulness" (v. 11). Love and productivity are, again, linked. Philemon brims with hidden emotional labor.

Love works: Love, faith, and labor

One model for emotional labor is the ecclesiastical expectation surrounding spiritual labor within Christianity. In the letter to Philemon, these strands meet and weave.

As we have seen, even Philemon is praised in this letter because his love brings refreshment to others. The voice of the letter to Philemon is confident of Philemon's obedience. It articulates the central thesis of emotional labor in vv. 8–9 and again in v. 14 as well as v. 21. Philemon is to obey not from obligation but from love, and he is to do so in ways that exceed expectations. Obedience is not enough; Philemon must exceed the mark and must do so because he wants to. What Philemon might actually want, what Philemon might feel, like the wants and feelings and needs of Onesimus, is never even asked or addressed in the letter.

But there is more hidden labor besides, and much of it affective. As I alluded to earlier in this chapter, Philemon exists for us to read because of thousands of hours of quiet, anonymous, hidden labor of scribes, textual critics, translators, and more. These were supported by tens of thousands of teachers, counselors, and clergy. They live and work in buildings tended and supported by the labor of millions of laity and patrons. Philemon exists for us to read because of hidden, affective labor.

This letter about hidden labor and affect, through the hidden love-laden labor of anonymous millions, ends up erasing the letter writer as well, whether the letter was really written by Paul or someone writing in Paul's name. The letter writer's real intention and desire vanish beneath the weight of commentary, homily, and scholarship. If the letter is pseude-pigraphic, the real Paul is being erased in this letter of labor with words through the appropriation of his name three times, including that of his handwriting as a pledge to return or repay a favor (vv. 1, 9, 19). But even without resorting to pseudepigraphy, the contents themselves quickly overwhelm Paul with questions of labor and love. Paul's own agenda is swiftly lost; it becomes unknown and unknowable as "work" and "useful-ness" in various ways become the foci of those reading the letter. In other words, Paul is erased by his own call for affective labor. The letter writer becomes the fantasy of the affected, emotional laborer: the one individual whose feelings are fully realized, the one individual who truly gets to feel and act on those feelings, the one individual who is fully seen. But the letter writer or the "Paul" that appears is, in many ways, the reader's own reflection. The letter's call for fellowship or *koinōnia* (v. 6) turns out to be decidedly hierarchical and bulwarked by emotion and emotional labor. But "Paul" also becomes the cypher and model for life as imagined at the top of the hierarchy. Paul becomes the reader's fantasy-self.

Conclusion

So the themes of Philemon fuse. The letter is a complicated soup of ideas: love, service, devotion, obedience, duty, usefulness, and labor. Labor and love are merged and emerge throughout the letter. Debt, both moral and material, and the embodiment of debt in service (slavery?) and impris-onment are pervasive. Love and obligation merge time and again, as does service, constraint, request, and command. Whether Onesimus is free or enslaved, servant or lover, congregant or brother, in the letter to Philemon, love is always compulsory and affect is always effective.

The letter to Philemon is, therefore, a troubling one in terms of both context and characterization. Onesimus, the purported raison d'etre, is scarcely present. The principal characters are otherwise unknown. Even "Paul," despite the thrice repetition of his name and showing off his own hand (vv. 1, 9, 19), can't be seen for certain in the dim thicket of the letter's words. When we remove the characters of "Paul," Philemon, and Onesimus from the letter to Philemon, we are left with only its language promoting emotional labor, the affect of service to others. All that is clear is a generic command to serve and the confidence that this service will be done out of love, not command. The institution of slavery, the emotions of service, and the illusion of domestic love—these three are all that remain. Invisible service—slavery?—becomes the symbol of our *koinōnia*, the central metaphor for faith in "Paul," and now the paradigm for emotional labor in late capitalism. In the end, the words and work of the letter to Philemon erase us all.

Conclusion

Letters Lost in the Mail

Commentary and/as story: On the building of backgrounds

Philemon is a brief document, but it develops themes of labor, family, domesticity, and love. It is explicit in places, replete with names, but it is powerfully vague in others, unclear even what its central entreaty on Onesimus's behalf might include. It is a private letter that has earned canonical status.

And it is extremely elusive to the commentator.

Together, we have reviewed the content of the letter very closely, only to find that it leaves more questions than answers. A letter is an active, living act of communication. It is a moment—but only a moment—of a longer and larger conversation. It depends upon context to be fully sensible.

We have reviewed some potential contexts for Philemon, surveying the main lines that have been suggested by scholarship so far. Philemon, early on, was largely neglected by readers of Paul until John Chrysostom developed a series of homilies based upon it. Chrysostom, wanting to perpetuate a view of Christianity that was both reformist (reducing slave abuse) and socially conservative (acknowledging the political and economic reality of his day), articulated a context for Philemon: Paul was returning an escaped slave, Onesimus.

Chrysostom's narrative certainly "works," but, as we have seen, it is based upon several assumptions—assumptions which incline a commentator to certain interpretive moves among and along Philemon's sometimes tortured syntax. Other reconstructions also "work," including readings that see either Paul desiring a slave as an assistant or the entire question of slavery as a commentator's invention and intrusion. Scholarship of the nineteenth and twentieth century problematized Chrysostom's reconstruction largely by revealing how much it depends upon conjecture and how equally plausible alternative background narratives can be posited.

Indeed, in our survey of options proposed, we have seen that the following interpretive contexts "work" equally well: Paul was returning an escaped Onesimus; Paul was returning a still enslaved Onesimus; Paul was refusing the gift of a would-be patron; Paul was requesting the return of Onesimus to Paul's service; Onesimus was not a slave at the time of Paul's writing; Paul was not writing to Philemon but to Archippus; Onesimus and Philemon were brothers; Onesimus and Archippus were brothers; Onesimus and Philemon went on, ultimately to be forgotten; Onesimus went on to become a bishop and was the hidden hand behind the collection of Paul's letters.

Each of these proposed contexts requires some conjecture. Each can also be defended from the content of Philemon and from knowledge of the ancient world. Each makes a return to Philemon sensible through a rereading of the letter with the reconstructed context in mind. Major themes and ideas from the letter clearly emerge. The letter, jewel-like, reflects and refracts the light of the Greco-Roman social and cultural history of the first-century empire.

Most of these readings, however, are incompatible; many are direct refutations of another. It is the general practice of commentators, when this emerges, to pick one reading, throw one's weight behind it and, for better or worse, stake a claim. I will not.

Instead, I will reassert that interpreting the letter depends upon the reconstruction of its context, and the reconstruction of its context will vary based upon the commentator. Commentary is, when one thinks about it, much more about generation of plausible meanings than it is the elimination of probable meanings via the articulation of a single, final reading. Commentary is a process of creating literary worlds through rereading. These rereadings reflect the needs, limits, energies, and ambitions of the commentator. Commentary is not arbitrary. It must conform to the strictures of the words—and often *worlds*—of the text under review. But it is also neither singular nor final.

Instead of resolving the differences we have found, I want to return to our initial metaphor, a letter found in a library, reading a document that floats freely through the world of Western literature, unmoored. We have taken each character, in turn, as a focus: Onesimus and the world of ancient slavery; Philemon, the *kurios*, and his possible household; Paul and the question of pseudepigraphy, the ultimate "death of the author." Each character has, for a moment at least, vanished or become central. We have seen how, again and again, the letter to Philemon has entered grand debates of the West. Philemon was critical in establishing Paul and Christianity as a religious community that could effect (slight) change but also conform to social norms. Philemon was critical to debates leading up to the American Civil War and the abolition of modern slavery. Philemon reflects an emerging understanding of ancient Roman sexual and social mores and values. Philemon awakens questions about hidden labor, slavery reparation, and emotional labor. Philemon does this precisely because it cannot be fully contained or tamed by a commentator's final word or conclusion. Commentary requires context. The context of Philemon is built from the bricks of the text's language and larger cultural and historic setting cemented by the commentator's own knowledge, access, and social location. Commentary is generative of meaning, not exclusionary. It is retelling, not telling. It is rereading, not reading.

Reading Philemon again for the first time

Rereading Philemon has renewed my attention to the hidden labor of the ancient slave and the real mar slavery left upon the achievements—all the achievements—of the ancient world. It reminds me as well that this mar is not absent from my own modern world. The economy of Great Britain was ballooned in the early colonial age by investments in slave trade. The United States was founded and built upon the backs of slaves, the legacy of which is still felt today. Slavery is not just a historic phenomenon. Slavery still exists; human trafficking still continues, particularly affecting the world's most poor, defenseless, and weak.

Rereading Philemon has renewed my attention to the question of race, reparation, class, and hidden, often emotional, labor in the world around me. I notice the absent Onesimus, a character made flat by the letter writer's disinterest. Despite the letter's cloying paternalism and grandiose claims ("my very heart"), all we learn about Onesimus is his conversion (at least as he assured his patron[s]) and his "usefulness." Was Onesimus really a convert, or a slave once again looking for the master's favor? Did Onesimus want to go back or was this his patron's idea? What services (one is tempted to use scare quotes) did Onesimus perform for Philemon or for "Paul"? Was he Philemon's slave or brother? Did Onesimus have debts, or did he have a claim for reparations, along with every other slave and slave descendent? Who owes their life to whom?

Rereading Philemon calls me to these questions and to others regarding the hidden labor around me today. Who emptied the trash can in my office on campus? Are they well? What do they feel and desire? Why do they work for my college? Do they like it? Why or why not? Philemon calls me to think about the "useful" people in my life and to ask if I am treating them ethically.

Rereading Philemon reminds me of the complex engagement of love and labor. It makes me think about the effects of affect around me. It makes me want to attend more to the emotional laborers who care for me now and will likely care for me and my loved ones in the future. It makes me want to be more attentive to the labor inequities that I encounter on every trip to the market, mall, theater, or restaurant. It makes me want to rethink encounters with administrators, bureaucrats, clerks, technical support, and customer service workers. It makes me want to clarify my responsibilities to my students and to help junior colleagues do the same.

Rereading Philemon, even with the irresolvable but always permeable dynamics of commentary and interpretation, has awakened all these issues, themes, ideas, and moments for application. Of course, one may readily point out: these are also, also, very much the issues of the modern world of late capitalism, including the epistemological uncertainty, the concern over social value as productivity, the concern over affect and emotional labor, the neo-Marxist concern over wage inequity and the struggle of neoliberal economies, attention to social privilege, racial and ethnic disparity, historic and contemporary. Like all the other commentators, these questions I have found in Philemon are merely the questions of my own day, imposed upon the book.

Yes.

And, so, the reading and rereading of letters continues, defiantly making meanings, again and again, out of the very substance of its hiddenness and vagary.

Works Cited

Ahmed, Sara. 2004. *The Cultural Poetics of Emotion* (New York: Routledge).

Ahmed, Sara. 2010. *The Promise of Happiness* (Durham, NC: Duke University Press).

Artz-Grabner, Peter. 2001. "The Case of Onesimos: An Interpretation of Paul's Letter to Philemon Based on Documentary Papyri and Ostraca," *Annali di storia dell'esegesi* 18: 589–614.

Ashforth, Blake E. and Roland H. Humphrey. 1993. "Emotional Labor in Service Roles: The Influence of Identity," *Academy of Management Review* 18: 88–115.

Avalos, Hector. 2011. *Slavery, Abolition and the Ethics of Biblical Scholarship* (Sheffield: Sheffield Phoenix).

Barclay, John M. G. 1991. "Paul, Philemon and the Dilemma of Christian Slave Ownership," *New Testament Studies* 37: 161–86.

Barth, Markus and Helmut Blanke. 2000. *The Letter to Philemon: A New Translation with Notes and Commentary* (Grand Rapids, MI: Wm. Eerdmans).

Barthes, Roland. 1968. "The Death of the Author," in *Image-Music-Text* (ed. and trans. Stephen Heath; New York: Hill and Wang), 142–48.

Barton, Carlin. 1993. *The Sorrows of the Ancient Romans: The Gladiator and the Monster* (Princeton, NJ: Princeton University Press).

Baur, Ferdinand C. 1875. *Paul, the Apostle of Jesus Christ, His Life and Work, His Epistles and His Doctrine: A Contribution to the Critical History of Primitive Christianity* (ed. Eduard Zeller; trans. A. Menzies; London: Williams and Norgate).

Birdsall, J. Neville. 1993. "Presbytēs in Philemon 9: A Study in Conjectural Emendation," *New Testament Studies* 39: 625–30.

Bitner, M., B. H. Booms and M. S. Tetrault. 1990. "The Service Encounter: Diagnosing Favorable and Unfavorable Incidents," *Journal of Marketing* 54: 71–84.

Bömer, Franz. 1958–63. *Untersuchungen über die Religion der Slaven in Griechenland und Rom* (4 vols; Mainz: Verlag der Akademie die Wissenschaft und die Literatur).

Bradley, Keith R. 1990. "*Servus Onerosus*: Roman Law and the Troublesome Slave," *Slavery and Abolition* 11: 135–57.

Bradley, Keith R. 1994. *Slavery and Society in Rome* (New York: Cambridge University Press).

Bradley, Keith R. 2000. "Animalizing the Slave: The Truth of Fiction," *Journal of Roman Studies* 90: 110–25.

Bruce, Frederick F. 1984. *The Epistles to the Colossians, to Philemon, and to the Ephesians* (Grand Rapids, MI: Eerdmans).

Bulan, Heather F., R. Erickson and A. Wharton. 1997. "Doing for Others on the Job: The Affective Requirements of Service Work, Gender and Emotional Well-Being," *Social Problems* 44: 235–56.

Byron, John. 2004. "Paul and the Background of Slavery: The *Status Quaestionis* in New Testament Scholarship," *Currents in Research: Biblical Studies* 3: 116–39.

Callahan, Allen D. 1993. "Paul's Epistle to Philemon: Toward an Alternative Argumentum," *Harvard Theological Review* 86: 357–76.

Callahan, Allen D. 1995. "John Chrysostom on Philemon: A Response to Margaret M. Mitchell," *Harvard Theological Review* 88: 149–56.

Callahan, Allen D. 1997. *Embassy of Onesimus: The Letter of Paul to Philemon* (Valley Forge, PA: Trinity).

Callahan, Allen D. 1998. " 'Brother Saul': An Ambivalent Witness to Freedom," in Callahan, Horsley and Smith, 1998: 235–50.

Callahan, Allen D. and Richard A. Horsley. 1998. "Slave Resistance in Classical Antiquity," in Callahan, Horsley and Smith, 1998: 133–52.

Callahan, Allen D., Richard A. Horsley and Abraham Smith. 1998. "Introduction: The Slavery of New Testament Studies," in Callahan, Horsley and Smith, 1998: 1–18.

Callahan, Allen D., Richard A. Horsley and Abraham Smith (eds). 1998. *Slavery in Text and Interpretation* (*Semeia*, 83/84; Atlanta: Society of Biblical Literature).

Church, F. Forrester. 1978. "Rhetorical Structure and Design in Paul's Letter to Philemon," *Harvard Theological Review* 71: 17–33.

Connolly, A. L. 1987. "Onesimos," in *New Documents Illustrating Early Christianity IV* (ed. G. H. R. Horsley; North Ryde, NSW: Macquarie University), 179–81.

Coursar, Charles B. 2009. *Philippians and Philemon: A Commentary* (Louisville, KY: Westminster/John Knox).

Danker, Frederik W., Walter Bauer, William F. Arndt and F. Wilbur Gingrich. 2000. *Greek-English Lexicon of the New Testament and Other Early Christian Literature* (Chicago: University of Chicago Press, 3rd edn).

Duff, A. M. 1958. *Freedmen in the Early Roman Empire* (Cambridge: Heffer, 2nd edn).

Dunn, James D. G. 1996. *The Epistles to the Colossians and to Philemon* (Carlisle: Paternoster).

Edwards, Katie (ed.). 2015. *Rethinking Biblical Literacy* (New York: Bloomsbury).

Ehrman, Bart D. 2013. *Forgery and Counterforgery: The Use of Literary Deceit in Early Christian Polemics* (New York: Oxford University Press).

Elliott, Scott S. 2011. "'Thanks but No Thanks': Tact, Persuasion, and Negotiation of Power in Paul's Letter to Philemon," *New Testament Studies* 57: 51–64.

Engberg-Pedersen, Troels. 2000. *Paul and the Stoics* (Louisville, KY: Westminster John Knox).

Fitzmyer, Joseph A. 2000. *The Letter to Philemon* (New York: Doubleday).

Frilingos, Chris. 2000. "'For My Child Onesimus': Paul and Domestic Power in Philemon," *Journal of Biblical Literature* 119: 91–104.

Gamble, Harry. 1975. "The Redaction of the Pauline Letters and the Formation of the Pauline Corpus," *Journal of Biblical Literature* 94: 403–18.

Glancy, Jennifer A. 2006. *Slavery in Early Christianity* (Minneapolis, MN: Fortress).

Goodenough, Erwin R. 1929. "Paul and Onesimus," *Harvard Theological Review* 22: 181–83.

Goodenough, Erwin R. 1933. *The Meaning of Ephesians* (Chicago: University of Chicago Press).

Gregg, Melissa and Gregory J. Seigworth (eds). 2010. *The Affect Theory Reader* (Durham, NC: Duke University Press).

Harrill, J. A. 1999. "Using the Roman Jurists to Interpret Philemon: A Response to Peter Lampe," *Zeitschrift für die neutestamentliche Wissenschaft* 90: 135–38.

Harrill, J. A. 2000. "The Use of the New Testament in the American Slave Controversy: A Case History in the Hermeneutical Tension between Biblical Criticism and Christian Moral Debate," *Religion and American Culture* 10: 149–86.

Harris, Murray J. 2010. *Colossians and Philemon* (Nashville, TN: B & H Academic).

Harrison, Percy N. 1950. "Onesimus and Philemon," *Anglican Theological Review* 32: 268–94.

Hennig-Thurau, Thorsten, Markus Groth, Michael Paul and Dwayne D. Gremier. 2006. "Are All Smiles Created Equal? How Emotional Contagion and Emotional Labor Affect Service Relationships," *Journal of Marketing* 70: 58–73.

Hochschild, Arlie R. 1983. *The Managed Heart: Commercialization of Human Feelings* (Berkeley: University of California Press).

Hopkins, Keith. 1993. "Novel Evidence for Roman Slavery," *Past & Present* 138: 3–27.

Horsley, Richard A. 1998. "The Slave Systems of Classical Antiquity and Their
    Reluctant Recognition by Modern Scholars," in Callahan, Horsley and
    Smith, 1998: 19–66.

Jeal, Roy R. 2015. *Exploring Philemon: Freedom, Brotherhood and Partnership
    in the New Society* (Atlanta: Society of Biblical Literature).

Johnson, Matthew, James Noel, and Demetrius Williams (eds). 2012. *Onesimus
    Our Brother: Reading Religion, Race & Culture in* Philemon (Minneapolis,
    MN: Fortress).

Joshel, Sandra R. 1986. "Nurturing the Master's Child: Slavery and the Roman
    Child Nurse," *Signs: A Journal of Women in Culture and Society* 12: 3–22.

Joshel, Sandra R. 1992. *Work, Identity and Legal Status at Rome*
    (Norman: University of Oklahoma Press).

Knox, John. 1937. "Philemon and the Authenticity of Colossians," *Journal of
    Religion* 17: 144–60.

Knox, John. 1955. "The Epistle to Philemon: Introduction and Exegesis,"
    in *The Interpreter's Bible* (ed. George Arthur Buttrick; 12 vols; Nashville,
    TN: Abingdon Press), 9.553–73.

Knox, John. 1959. *Philemon among the Letters of Paul: A New View of Its Place
    and Importance* (Nashville, TN: Abingdon, rev. edn).

Koch, Eldon W. 1963. "A Cameo of Koinonia: The Letter to Philemon,"
    Interpretation 17: 183–87.

Koosed, Jennifer and Stephen D. Moore. 2014a. "Introduction: From Affect to
    Exegesis," *Biblical Interpretation* 22: 381–87.

Koosed, Jennifer and Stephen D. Moore (eds). 2014b. *Affect Theory and the
    Bible* (Special Issue). *Biblical Interpretation* 22: 381–528.

Kotrosits, Maia. 2015. *Rethinking Early Christian Identity: Affect, Violence, and
    Belonging* (Minneapolis, MN: Fortress).

Kreitzer, Larry J. 2008. *Philemon* (Sheffield: Sheffield Phoenix).

Kristeva, Julia. 1980. *Desire in Language: A Semiotic Approach to Language and
    Art* (ed. Leon S. Roudiez; trans. Thomas Gora, Alice Jardine and Leon S.
    Roudiez; New York: Columbia University Press).

Lampe, Peter. 2010. "Affects and Emotions in the Rhetoric of Paul's Letter
    to Philemon: A Rhetorical Psychological Interpretation," in *Philemon in
    Perspective: Interpreting a Pauline Letter* (ed. D. Francois Tolmie; Berlin: De
    Gruyter), 61–77.

Lewis, Lloyd A. 1991. "An African American Appraisal of the Philemon-
    Paul-Onesimus Triangle," in *Stony the Road We Trod: African American
    Biblical Interpretation* (ed. Cain Hope Felder; Minneapolis, MN: Augsburg
    Fortress), 232–46.

Lightfoot, J. B. 1916. *Saint Paul's Epistles to the Colossians and to Philemon: A Revised Text with Introduction, Notes, and Dissertations* (London: Macmillan).

Lohmeyer, Ernst. 1964. *Der Briefe an die Philipper, and die Kolosser und an Philemon* (Göttingen: Vandenhoeck & Ruprecht, 13th edn).

Lohse, Eduard. 1971. *Colossians and Philemon* (ed. Helmut Koester; trans. William R. Poehlmann and Robert J. Karris; Philadelphia: Fortress).

Marchal, Joseph A. 2011. "The Usefulness of Onesimus: The Sexual Use of Slaves and Paul's Letter to Philemon," *Journal of Biblical Literature* 130.4: 749–70.

Martin, Dale B. 1990. *Slavery as Salvation: The Metaphor of Slavery in Pauline Christianity* (New Haven, CT: Yale University Press).

Martin, Ralph P. 1991. *Ephesians, Colossians, and Philemon* (Louisville, KY: John Knox).

Martyn, J. L. 1997. *Galatians* (New York: Doubleday).

Mendelsohn, Isaac. 1949. *Slavery in the Ancient Near East: A Comparative Study of Slavery in Babylonia, Assyria, Syria, and Palestine from the Middle of the Third Millennium to the End of the First Millennium* (New York: Oxford University Press).

Metzger, Bruce M. 1987. *The Canon of the New Testament: Its Origin, Development and Significance* (New York: Oxford University Press).

Mitchell, Margaret M. 1995. "John Chrysostom and Philemon: A Second Look," *Harvard Theological Review* 88: 135–48.

Morrison, Larry R. 1980–81. "The Religious Defense of American Slavery before 1830," *Journal of Religious Thought* 37: 16–29.

Morrow, Glenn R. 1939. *Plato's Law on Slavery and Its Relation to Greek Laws* (Urbana: Illinois University Press).

Nordling, John G. 1991. "Onesimus Fugitivus: A Defense of the Runaway Slave Hypothesis in Philemon," *Journal for the Study of the New Testament* 41: 97–119.

Nordling, John G. 2004. *Philemon: A Theological Exposition of Sacred Scripture* (St Louis, MO: Concordia Publishing House).

Parker, David C. 2008. *An Introduction to the New Testament Manuscripts and Their Texts* (Cambridge: Cambridge University Press).

Patterson, Orlando. 1982. *Slavery and Social Death: A Comparative Study* (Cambridge, MA: Harvard University Press).

Patterson, Orlando. 1998. "Paul, Slavery and Freedom: Personal and Socio-Historical Reflections," in Callahan, Horsley and Smith, 1998: 263–79.

Pearson, Brook W. R. 1999. "Assumptions in the Criticism and Translation of Philemon," in *Translating the Bible: Problems and Prospects* (ed. Stanley E. Porter and Richard Hess; Sheffield: Sheffield Academic), 253–80.

Petersen, Norman R. 1985. *Rediscovering Paul: Philemon and the Sociology of Paul's Narrative World* (Philadelphia: Fortress).

Rapske, Brian M. 1991. "The Prisoner Paul in the Eyes of Onesimus," *New Testament Studies* 37: 187–203.

Roetzel, Calvin J. 1998. *The Letters of Paul: Conversations in Context* (Louisville, KY: Westminster John Knox, 4th edn).

Russell, David M. 1998. "The Strategy of a First-Century Appeals Letter: A Discourse Reading of Paul's Epistle to Philemon," *Journal of Translation and Textlinguistics* 11: 1–25.

Schaefer, Donovan O. 2015. *Religious Affects: Animality, Evolution and Power* (Durham, NC: Duke University Press).

Schaff, Phillip. 1994. *Nicene and Post-Nicene Fathers. Volume 9: Works of St. Chrysostom,* On the Priesthood, Ascetic Treatises, Select Homilies and Letters, Homilies on the Statues (Peabody: Hendrickson).

Sedgwick, Eve Kosofsky. 2011. *The Weather in Proust* (ed. Jonathan Goldberg; Durham, NC: Duke University Press).

Seesengood, Robert Paul. 2010. *Paul: A Brief History* (New York: Wiley-Blackwell).

Sokolowski, Franciszek. 1954. "Fees and Taxes in Greek Cults," *Harvard Theological Review* 47: 153–69.

Stark, Rodney. 2007. *Discovering God: The Origins of the Great Religions and the Evolution of Belief* (San Francisco: HarperOne).

Stower, Stanley K. 1986. *Letter Writing in Greco-Roman Antiquity* (Louisville, KY: Westminster John Knox).

Tomkins, Silvan. 1962–92. *Affect, Imagination, Consciousness* (4 vols; New York: Springer).

Urbach, Ephraim E. 1964. "The Laws Regarding Slavery as a Source for Social History of the Second Temple, the Mishnah and Talmud," in *Papers of the Institute of Jewish Studies, London* (ed. J. G. Weiss; Jerusalem: Magnes), 1–94.

Ville, Georges. 1981. *La Gladiature en occident des origenes à a la mort de Domitien* (Rome: École française de Rome).

Vogt, Joseph. 1974. *Ancient Slavery and the Ideal of Man* (Oxford: Blackwell).

Vos, Craig S. de. 2001. "Once a Slave, Always a Slave? Slavery, Manumission and Rational Patterns in Paul's Letter to Philemon," *Journal for the Study of the New Testament* 82: 89–105.

Wills, Lawrence M. 1998. "The Depiction of Slavery in the Ancient Novel," in Callahan, Horsley and Smith, 1998: 113–32.

Winter, Sara. 1987. "Paul's Letter to Philemon," *New Testament Studies* 33: 1–15.

Wire, Antoinette C. 1990. *The Corinthian Women Prophets: A Reconstruction through Paul's Rhetoric* (Minneapolis, MN: Fortress).

Zahn, Theodor. 1879. *Introduction to the New Testament.* Trans. J. M. Trout et al. New York: Scribner.

Index of Biblical References

Index of Subjects

www.ingramcontent.com/pod-product-compliance
Ingram Content Group UK Ltd.
Pitfield, Milton Keynes, MK11 3LW, UK
UKHW020703280225
455688UK00004B/233